A Newbies Guide to iPhone 8

The Unofficial Handbook to iPhone and iOS 10 (Includes iPhone 5, 5s, 5c, iPhone 6, 6 Plus, 6s, 6s Plus, iPhone SE, iPhone 7 ,7 Plus, iPhone 8, and iPhone 8 Plus)

Minute Help Press
SOME PEOPLE ONLY HAVE A FEW MINUTES TO SPARE

Minute Help Press

www.minutehelp.com

© 2017. All Rights Reserved.

Table of Contents

Table of Contents

Introduction

Are you the proud owner of a new iPhone 8 or iPhone 8 Plus? Congratulations! Apple's iPhone is an incredible piece of personal technology that brings your work, play, education, and more into the palm of your hand. The latest version of iPhone is the iPhone 8, which is available in regular and Plus sizes. The iPhone 8 Plus is a much larger version of the iPhone 8. The regular 8 includes a 4.7-inch HD retina display with a 1334 x 750 pixel resolution, while the 8 Plus sports a massive 5.5-inch HD retina display with a 1920 x 1080 resolution. In other words, the 8 Plus is bigger and sharper, but the regular iPhone 8 is no slouch in the display department!

Like the 7 Plus, the iPhone 8 and 8 Plus include optical image stabilization, but the new features don't stop there. Both phones include a 12MP camera with f/1.8 aperture and six-element lens, allowing you to take even better photos. The iPhone 8 Plus gives you the ultimate photo taking experience with dual lenses. The latest innovation is the Apple-designed Image Signal Processor (ISP). This brings better pixel processing, faster low-light auto focus and noise reduction. With all of these new features, you will look like a professional photographer at the touch of a button. With a f/1.8 aperture and six-element lens, you can take even better photos no matter which of these iPhones you use.

Both models are available in space gray, silver and an all-new gold, and both of them are just as beautiful on the inside as they are on the surface. With a blazingly fast A10 processor and a new M10 motion coprocessor that not only keeps track of your elevation, steps taken, and distances traveled, but also tracks the pace of your run or walk and makes it possible for Siri to stay on without compromising your battery, iPhone has never been faster or more efficient. iPhone 8 and 8 Plus also sport a camera that will shoot 1080p HD video and take 12MP stills (plus a slew of other features, like Retina Flash for selfies).

iPhone 8 and 8 Plus focuses on wireless technology and retains a major change – the removal of the 3.5 mm headphone jack at the bottom of the phone. EarPods, still included with your new phone, will now use a Lighting connector; or, you can opt to purchase the new wireless AirPods.

Both the iPhone 8 and the iPhone 8 Plus ship with iOS 10, the newest version of Apple's iOS mobile operating system. iOS 10 looks very similar to iOS 9 on the surface, but it's full of new features and improvements that Apple users have been lusting after for years. Building on iOS 9, iOS 10 includes improved 3D Touch technology that is even more useful, updated built-in apps like News, Notes, Wallet, and iCloud Drive, keyboard improvements that make typing on a hand-held screen effortless and intuitive, added enhancements to Messages that include the ability to handwrite notes, share images, and video, a more powerful and more intelligent iteration of Siri, intelligent suggestions for searches and common actions based on your lifestyle and habits, a number of small design tweaks that add up to a vastly improved user experience, beefed up security features, and much, much more. In other words, iPhones running iOS 10 are even more fun, useful, social and easy to use than ever.

The biggest innovation of all? The iPhone 8 and iPhone 8 Plus now feature wireless charging. It will charge more quickly, too! Apple has finally added wired quick charging and Qi-compatible wireless charging. Add the new glass casing in exchange for the old aluminum one, and you have one impressive leap in technology.

A note about storage. The iPhone 7 and 7 Plus featured 32GB and 128GB of storage, but the iPhone 8 and 8 Plus have doubled that, at 64GB and 256BG! That's great news for those who like to store a lot of music or songs on their phones. Another innovation for song lovers? The iPhone 8 gives you a 25% boost in volume compared to the iPhone 7's stereo speakers.

If you're unsure of what any of this means for you, no worries! We've written this guide just for you. While iPhone 8 is an impressive feat of technology and engineering, we'll skip the technical jargon and help you learn how to get the most out of your new iPhone in plain English. If you're new to iPhone or to iOS, we promise there's nothing to fear. iPhone is incredibly intuitive - with a handful of buttons and a few simple gestures, you'll gain access not only to a top-notch mobile phone, but also to a world of information, music, videos, games, connectivity, productivity, and more. And it gets better - we think you're going to have fun learning all this stuff!

If you're new to iOS (found on iPhone, iPod, and iPad), or if you're new to mobile computing altogether, this guide will help you get started with iPhone and iOS 10 quickly and easily. Even if you've used older versions of iPhone or iOS, you'll find plenty of new ways to learn, work, play, and share with iPhone 8. We'll show you how to set up and customize your iPhone, use all of the pre-installed apps like an expert, keep your iPhone healthy and happy, and discover some of the best free and nearly free third party apps available in the Apple App Store. Along the way, we'll give you plenty of easy-to-follow instructions, screenshots, tips, and tricks that will have you tapping, swiping, syncing, and sharing like a pro in no time.

About This Guide

This guide is designed for novices and advanced iPhone/iOS users alike. The tips and instructions here are tailored to the iPhone 8 / iPhone 8 Plus and iOS 10, but you'll find plenty of relevant information for older iPhone models and older versions of the software. Just be aware that iPhone 8 and iOS 10 have introduced quite a few new features that may not be available on older iPhones!

We've broken things down into six major parts. **Part 1: Meet Your iPhone** will help you unpack the box, learn how to interact with your iPhone, and glide through the set-up process. **Part 2: Getting to Know Your iPhone** will introduce you to the basic features and navigational system of the device. **Part 3: Mastering Your Pre-installed Apps** will walk you through the twenty-eight pre-installed apps in detail to help you master what's available right out of the box. **Part 4: Making It Your Own** guides you through customization and personalization. **Part 5: Maintenance and Security** will help you keep your iPhone healthy and safe. Finally, **Part 6: Must-Have Apps for Your iPhone** includes a list of 53 of our favorite apps - we hope you enjoy them as much as we do!

There's a lot of information here, but don't feel like you need to absorb it all at once. Think of this guide as a friendly support system for you as you learn to use and enjoy this incredible piece of consumer technology. If you're new to iPhone or to iOS, start by reading through Parts 1 and 2. This should get you on your feet. Be sure to look at Part 5 to learn how to care for your new iPhone. You may want to use Parts 3, 4, and 6 as reference material. You can read them straight through from start to finish or just browse the table of contents for the information most helpful to you. These chapters will also be helpful for experienced users who want to get the most out of iPhone 8 and iOS 10 and will include our favorite tips for new iOS 10 features.

Few devices are as painless to use as the iPhone - we hope you have fun and enjoy the journey. Now let's get started!

About iPhone and iOS 10

The Apple iPhone is a mobile phone, but it's also much, much more. In addition to making calls, iPhone checks your email, gives you access to your social networking sites, helps you stay organized, connects you to the internet, and serves as an MP3 player, a handheld television, a camera, and a personal gaming system. If you've used an iPad or an iPod Touch, you're already familiar with the dazzling touchscreen technology that makes the iPhone so much fun to use. The keyboard appears on the touchscreen when needed, and instead of a mouse, you'll be using your finger. The iPhone can also register more than one simultaneous touch, which allows users to double tap and use other multitouch gestures. iPhone also includes a camera capable of taking still images and video, a built-in microphone and speaker, and Location Services (services that use cellular and wireless data and GPS to determine your iPhone's location).

As of October 2017, there have been seventeen major iPhone models - iPhone, iPhone 3G, iPhone 3GS, iPhone 4, iPhone 4S, iPhone 5, iPhone 5s, iPhone 5c, iPhone 6, iPhone 6 Plus, iPhone 6S, iPhone 6S Plus, iPhone SE, iPhone 7, iPhone 7 Plus, iPhone 8, and iPhone 8 Plus. The future iPhone X is just on the horizon! The first iPhone, released in 2007, connected to wireless internet networks, took still images, and, of course, made phone calls. It was soon replaced by the iPhone 3G - a model that actually used cellular networks to provide internet access. 3G access meant that you could get online anywhere your cellphone had a 3G signal from your wireless carrier. And things only got better from there. Later models of iPhone added video camera capabilities, a dual-facing camera, fingerprint security, an onboard motion coprocessor capable of passively tracking health and fitness data, and other improved features. And in September 2017, Apple released the best iPhone yet - the iPhone 8.

The software that supports all of this activity on your iPhone is an operating system called iOS 10. iOS 10 is the most current version of Apple's iOS, and it runs on newer iPads and iPod Touches, as well as on your iPhone 8. We'll refer to iOS 10 quite a bit throughout this guide, so you'll want to understand what we're talking about. Without getting too deep into specifics, think of your digital content as a really exotic pet, and the operating system as the specialized habitat that it lives in. Now, just like you wouldn't put a hamster wheel in a fish tank, you wouldn't install a Windows program on an iOS 10 device - in fact, you can't. When you're setting up your iOS 10 "habitat," you'll be populating it with apps (also known as programs to Windows users) designed especially for iOS devices. Fortunately, iOS devices make it easy to find iOS apps.

They're all located in the Apple App Store, and all you'll need is an Apple ID and a finger to access them.

The iOS 10 update focuses on unifying the iPhone's features and improving its contextual intelligence. This means that many of its new features aren't immediately apparent, though some - like Messages and Home features - are hard to miss. However, all of these features add up into a user experience that's smarter, more efficient, and better adapted to you as an individual than ever before.

But enough background already. Ready to see what all the fuss is about? Let's get that iPhone out of the box and into your hands!

Part 1: Meet Your iPhone

We're going to start at the very beginning by introducing some of the key concepts you'll need to get started, including what's in the box, the buttons and hardware on your new iPhone, and the ways you'll interact with your device, including actions and typing. Then, we'll walk through the setup process. You may find yourself referring back to the first few sections of this chapter as you move through setup and get started using your iPhone. If you feel like you're getting overwhelmed, you may want to skip ahead to 1.6: Setting Up Your iPhone, and then review the earlier sections when you're feeling a little more comfortable. In our experience, it's easiest to get the hang of using an iOS device by actually using one! Rest assured that your iPhone is designed to be easy to use, and it will happily tolerate beginner's mistakes. Feel free to play and experiment - we promise you won't break anything. Now let's get started!

1. What's in the Box

Your iPhone is ready to go right out of the box - no need to fully charge the battery or connect it to a computer. It really is as simple as turning it on and configuring some basic setup options. We'll walk you through the process in 1.6, but don't worry. This is about as simple as it gets.

When you open up your iPhone's box, you'll find the iPhone itself sitting on top. There's a protective plastic sticker covering the screen and the back of the device - go ahead and peel that off and discard it. Underneath the iPhone, you'll find a lightning to 3.5 mm Headphone Jack Adapter, Lightning to USB Cable, and USB Power Adapter. These represent the very latest in charging innovation!

The USB cable connects to the iPhone's power dock, located at the bottom of the device. If you've used older iPhones, you'll notice that the eight-pin "lightning dock" is a good deal smaller than the older thirty-pin version found in iPhone 4. It's also reversible, so you're guaranteed to get it plugged in right the first time! The other end connects to your computer's USB port and to the port on the power adaptor. Go ahead and figure out how everything connects - it's not tricky, but it's good to familiarize yourself with the process.

You'll also find an envelope with some of the most minimal documentation in existence - a card that labels the four buttons on the device, a product information guide with safety and legal notices, and a couple of Apple stickers. A word of warning: purchasing an iOS device has been known to lead to an excessive collection of Apple stickers.

And finally, you'll find one more goodie in your box - Apple's EarPod headphones. They're a great set of ear buds that include volume and playback control, and they come with their own carrying case! Unlike previous versions of EarPods, this version uses a Lighting Connector instead of relying on the 35 mm headphone jack, which has been removed. If you have old pairs of EarPods, don't worry. You'll also get a Lightning to 3.5 mm Headphone Jack Adapter in the box, so you can easily use any older EarPods that you already have on hand.

Before you discard your box, be sure to check with your wireless carrier about how to activate the phone - you'll likely need some of the numbers that are printed on the side to complete this process.

1.2 The iPhone Buttons

There are only five physical buttons on your iPhone, but you'll want to locate them right away and learn their names.

Sleep/Wake (On/Off)

Hold your iPhone in your hand so that the circular button is positioned under the screen. Now look at the right edge of the phone. You'll see a skinny rectangular button. That's your sleep/wake switch, which also moonlights as your on/off switch. If you've used older iPhones, you'll notice that this button has moved from the top of the device to the side - yes, there is an adjustment period, but we promise it'll feel normal eventually!

There are two ways to interact with this button. Press and hold it to power on your device. Press it briefly without holding it to put your iPhone to sleep, and again to wake it up. Putting your iPhone to sleep is sufficient to conserve battery power most of the time, but there may be times when you need to fully power off your device. To accomplish this, press and hold the button until the "slide to power off" message appears. Swipe the circle with the power icon on it to the right to power the device off, or tap the circle labeled Cancel if you've changed your mind (see 1.4 to learn about tapping and swiping). Go ahead and practice this a couple of times until you get the hang of it!

New to iOS 10 is the ability to Raise to Wake. If you have an iPhone 6S or later, you'll have the ability to easily wake your phone just by picking it up. This feature is automatically turned on in your new phone but can easily be turned off, if desired. This is another way that phones with iOS 10 can conserve battery power without having to use the Sleep/Wake button.

To turn on or off the Raise to Wake feature navigate to Settings. From there select Display & Brightness. Next to Auto-Lock, you'll see Raise to Wake. Toggle on or off, as needed.

Tip: To get the most out of Raise to Wake, combine it with a new feature that you can set up for the Home button (see 1.6), which allows you to unlock your phone without having to click the Home button.

Volume

The volume controls are located on the left edge of your iPhone, if you hold the device with the screen facing you. They work just like you'd expect – press the upper button to increase volume and the lower button to decrease it. You can also use the either volume button as a shutter for the camera app.

Mute Switch

Your iPhone's mute switch is located just above the volume controls. If a red stripe is showing, your iPhone is muted. It will still vibrate for incoming calls, messages and notifications, though you can adjust these settings if you like (see 4.2 and 4.6).

Home Button / Touch ID Sensor

This is a terrifically important button – it's the large circle centered beneath the screen. You can press this button to wake your iPhone up, and you'll also use it to return to your home screen (more on this in 2.1). The Home button also serves as a Touch ID sensor. Touch ID reads your fingerprint for an additional layer of security to your iPhone, as well as a boatload of convenience.

1.3 Other Hardware

Your iPhone is equipped with all kinds of gadgetry, though you'd never know it to look at the sleek device. Here's an outline of your iPhone's various ports and accessories.

Camera (Front and Back)

Your iPhone comes with a front-and rear-facing camera. It's tiny, but you can see the front camera just above the screen if you squint. The back camera's a little easier to find. It's the larger of the two circles on the back of your phone (the smaller circle is the camera flash).

If you have an iPhone 8 Plus, you will have two front-facing cameras, including a newly added dual rear camera.

Microphones and Speakers

Next to the front camera, you'll see a black line. This is the speaker you'll listen to during calls by holding it to your ear. There are more speakers on the bottom of the phone as well. iPhone 8 and 8 Plus still include stereo speakers in both locations making the sound on your phone even better.

The iPhone has two microphones. One is on the bottom of the phone - this microphone is the one you'll speak into when you make calls. The other microphone is on the back, between the camera and the flash. You'll be glad you have it to capture audio along with your video!

Antennas

Your iPhone's antennas are located on the back panel of your phone. There are two antennas in the iPhone 8 and 8 Plus. Unlike previous versions, these are hard to spot because Apple has worked to remove the antenna lines found on the back of your phone, making the design even cleaner and more streamlined.

Headphone Jack

The iPhone 8 and 8 Plus do not have a headphone jack, a major change from previous iPhones. If you're going to listen to audio content with headphones, you'll need to do so using the Lighting Connector (see below).

Lightning Connector

The nine-pin port at the bottom is where your USB cable connects to the device. Note that this is not the same thirty-pin connector used on older iPhones, iPads and iPods, and may require new accessories for users who skipped the iPhone 5 and 6 series upgrades.

The Lightning Connector also now serves as your headphone jack. Your new iPhone will come with EarPods that include a Lightning Connector. Because this is not a standard jack (3.5 mm), standard headphones, speaker cables, or older versions of EarPods will need to use the Headphone Jack Adapter that comes with your iPhone 8 or 8 Plus.

When you plug in a pair of headphones to an iOS 10 iPhone, your device will recognize them and suggest the most recent app you've used to listen to audio content (Music, Podcasts, Pandora, etc.).

SIM Tray

Your iPhone's SIM tray is located on the right side of the device (with the screen facing you). You'll need a special tool to open it (or, alternatively, a paper clip and some patience).

Multitouch Touchscreen with 3D Touch

We've saved the best for last. You have no doubt noticed your beautiful 4.7 inch (iPhone 8) or 5.5 inch (iPhone 8 Plus) touchscreen. For comparison's sake, the original iPhone screen measured 3.5 inches, and even the iPhone 5 only measured 4.0 inches. Your touchscreen will respond when you touch it, rotate it, tilt it, or shake it, and will dazzle you with its clarity, as you'll soon see. The iPhone 8 and 8 Plus have included even more useful and easy 3D Touch features for you to enjoy.

1.4 Finding Your Way Around

The iPhone is designed to be as intuitive as possible, and there are very few skills you'll need to master in order to use it. The touchscreen is simple; a few basic movements will allow you to navigate your iPhone smoothly and quickly. We've outlined the basic iPhone actions in this section for your reference.

Tap

This is the "click" of the iPhone world. A tap is just a brief touch. It doesn't have to be hard or last very long. You'll tap icons, hyperlinks, form choices, and more. You'll also tap numbers on a touch keypad in order to make calls. Don't worry, it's not rocket science!

Tap and Hold

This simply means touching the screen and leaving your finger in contact with the glass. It's useful for bringing up context menus or other options in some apps.

Double Tap

This refers to two rapid taps, like double clicking with your finger. Double tapping will perform different functions in different apps. It will also zoom in on pictures or webpages.

3D Touch: Press

3D Touch was a new feature in iPhone 6S and it adds an extra dimension to the way you interact with iPhone. With iPhone 8 and 8 Plus, 3D Touch is even better. This technology, first developed for the Apple Watch, allows you to use force in addition to position and duration. If you press the glass screen as though you were pressing a button, you can "peek" into items like Mail messages, previewing them without fully opening them. Then just press a little harder to "pop" the message open. Pressing other items will bring open a Quick Actions menu. For example, pressing the Camera icon will give you shortcuts to Take Selfie, Record Video, Record Slo-mo, and Take Photo, getting you to the app screen you want to use quickly. 3D Touch also plays into drawing apps, like the sketch feature in Notes. The amount of force you use affects the thickness of the line you draw on the screen. You can also turn your keyboard into a trackpad by using 3D Touch to select text when typing.

Whether you're already used to this feature from iPhone 7 or are getting to know it with your new iPhone 8, the 3D Touch feature is becoming even more ingrained in the way we use our devices, so we recommend getting on board with it now.

Swipe

Swiping means putting your finger on the surface of your screen and dragging it to a certain point and then removing your finger from the surface. You'll swipe to unlock or shut down your iPhone using a slider graphic. You'll also swipe to scroll up and down and from side to side, or to turn pages in a reading app. You'll use this motion to navigate through menu levels in your apps, through pages in Safari, and more. It'll become second nature overnight, we promise.

Drag

This is mechanically the same as swiping, but with a different purpose. You'll touch an object to select it, and then drag it to wherever it needs to go and release it. It's just like dragging and dropping with a mouse, but it skips the middleman.

Pinch

Take two fingers, place them on the iPhone screen, and move them either toward each other or away from each other in a pinching or reverse pinching motion. Moving your fingers together will zoom in inside many apps, including web browsers and photo viewers; moving them apart will zoom out.

Rotate and Tilt

Many apps on iPhone take advantage of rotating and tilting the device itself. For instance, in the paid app Star Walk, you can tilt the screen so that it's pointed at whatever section of the night sky you're interested in – Star Walk will reveal the constellations based on the direction the iPhone is pointed.

In most (but not all) apps and in your home screen, rotating the iPhone will cause the display to rotate its orientation in adjustment. This is great most of the time, but if you're reading a book in bed, it's possible to lock the orientation to prevent dizziness every time you shift position (see 2.6).

1.5 Typing on iPhone

iOS 9 introduced tremendous improvements to the iPhone's native onscreen keyboard, including the new San Francisco font found on the Apple Watch and a much clearer system for knowing whether or not the keyboard is going to output capital letters. Now, iOS 10 has built on these improvements and includes multilingual typing. This means you can use multiple languages in the same sentence or text without having to deal with pesky autocorrections.

To type on your iPhone, touch any field or area of the screen where you'd expect to be able to enter text. This brings up the iPhone keyboard. The first keyboard you see usually contains letters of the alphabet and some basic punctuation. iPhone is smart – it will automatically capitalize the first letter of a sentence, and you can hit the space bar twice to insert a period.

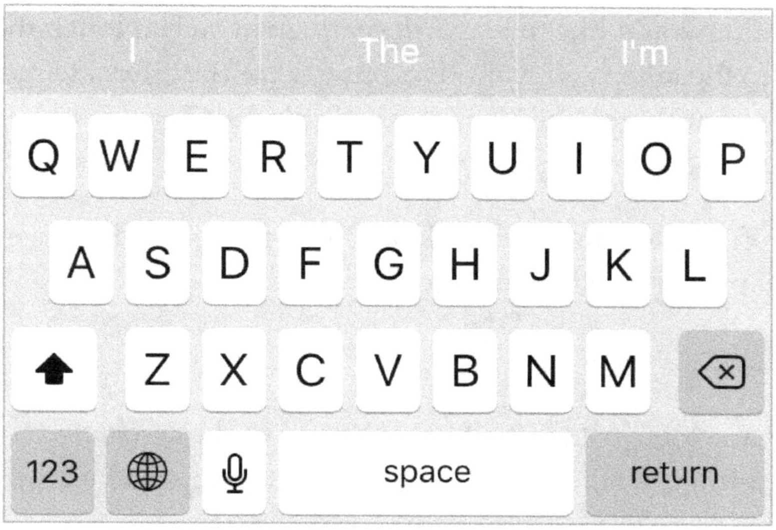

Screenshot 1: The iPhone's Alphabet Keyboard

There are a few things to notice on the keyboard – the delete key is marked with a little x (it's right next to the letter M), and the shift key is the key with the upward arrow (next to the letter Z).

By default, the first letter you type will be capitalized. You can tell what case the letters are in though at a quick glance.

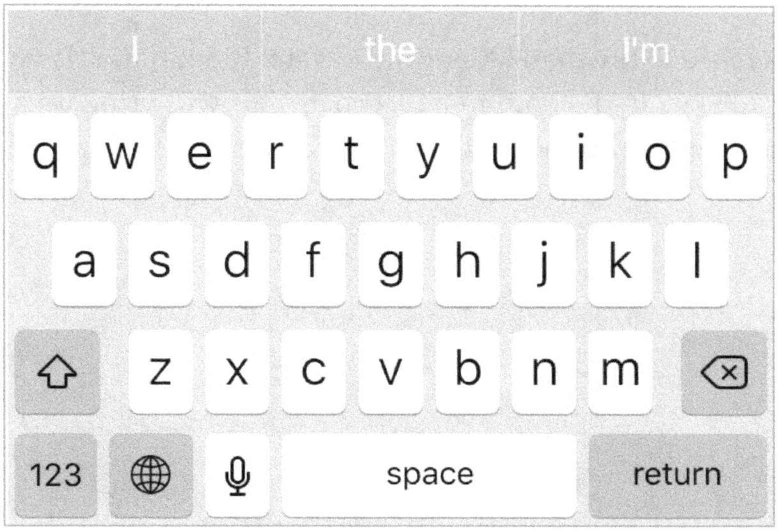

Screenshot 2: Lower Case Keyboard

Using the Shift Key

To use the shift key, just tap it and then tap the letter you want to capitalize or the alternate punctuation you'd like to use. Alternatively, you can touch the shift key and drag your finger to the letter you want to capitalize (or the alternate punctuation). When you release your finger, the character is displayed. Try this out a few times to see which method is the best for you.

Double tap the shift key to enter caps lock (a typing mode in which every letter is capitalized) and tap once to exit caps lock.

Special Characters

To type special characters, just tap and hold the key of the associated letter until options pop up. Drag your finger to the character you want to use, and be on your way.

Using Dictation

If you're really struggling with typing, you can always turn on Dictation and give your fingers a rest. Just tap the microphone key next to the space bar and start talking. Dictation also supports punctuation. For example, at the end of the sentence you simply say "period." It also understands several other punctuation marks. It's not perfect, but you'll likely be surprised at its accuracy.

Number and Symbol Keyboards

Of course, there's more to life than letters and exclamation marks. If you need to use numbers, tap the 123 key in the bottom left corner. This will bring up a different keyboard with numbers and punctuation.

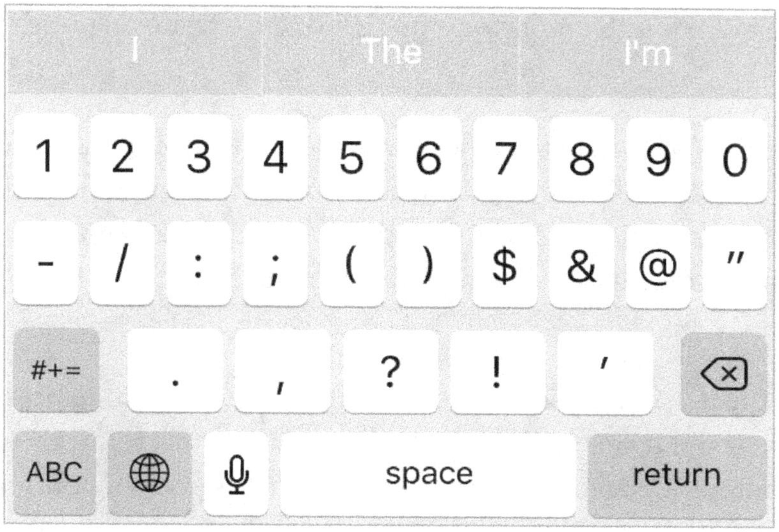

Screenshot 3: The Number and Punctuation Keyboard

From this keyboard, you can get back to the alphabet by tapping the ABC key in the bottom left corner. You can also access an additional keyboard which includes the remaining standard symbols by tapping the #+- key, just above the ABC key.

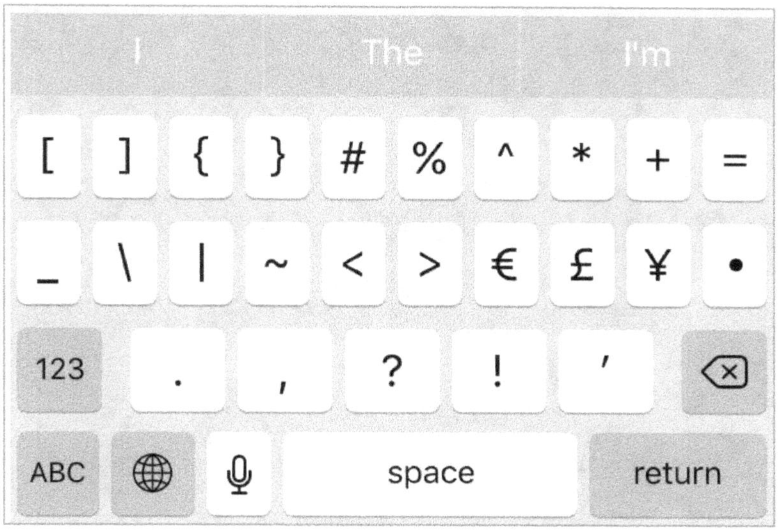

Screenshot 4: The Additional Symbol Keyboard

Emoji Keyboard

The emoji keyboard is accessible using the smiley face key between the 123 key and the dictation key. Emojis are tiny cartoon images that you can use to liven up your text messages or other written output. This goes far beyond the colon-based emoticons of yesteryear - there are enough emojis on your iPhone to create an entire visual vocabulary.

To use the emoji keyboard, note that there are categories along the bottom (and that the globe icon on the far left will return you to the world of language). Within those categories, there are several screens of pictographs to choose from. Many of the human emojis include multicultural variations. Just press and hold them to reveal other options.

Finally, if you're unsure what use emojis are if there's no way to express your love of tacos or unicorns, you'll be excited to see over 70 new emojis released with iOS 10 to use to your heart's content. Of course, if your love for emojis goes beyond the ones found in iOS 10, you can add stickers, third party apps, and enhanced emojis to express yourself (see 3.6).

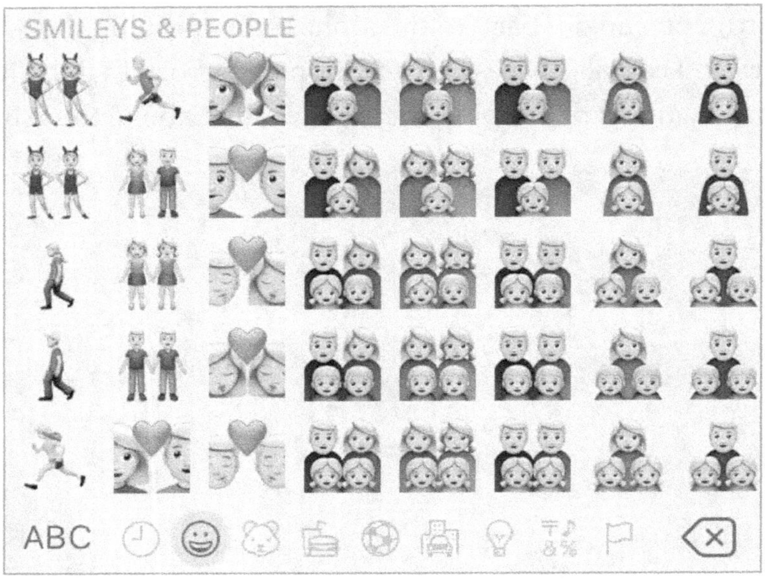

Screenshot 5: New Emoji Options on the Emoji Keyboard

New layout for iMessage stickers

You have new and wonderful ways of using stickers embedded in your conversations with iOS 10. Now, you can tap to send stickers in a thread, adjust the size, or place them on top of other stickers, bubbles, or photos. There is no coding required to build stickers. And using Xcode, you can turn your stickers into a pack that's ready to submit

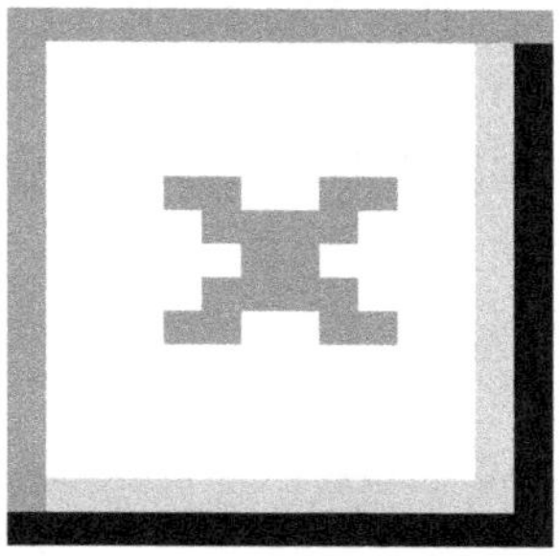

to the App Store.

Getting Started

Making sticker packs in iOS 10 is easy, and it can be done using your Mac, Apple ID, Sticker images, and Xcode. Download Xcode for free!

Images

You can create sticker packs using a set of image files in PNG, JPEG, or GIF format. You can also use animated images that are in APNG or GIF format.

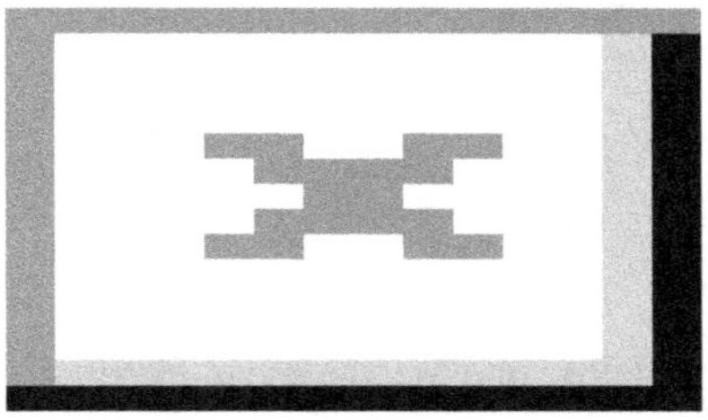

All About Tapback

Also new to iOS 10 is "Tapback", a new Messages app that allows you to insert an inline response as a visual icon. The action is faster and easier than ever. This is similar to using iMessage Stickers, in that the Tapback message icons are applied on top of the message, appearing inline within the conversation. Make sure that you have an updated version of iOS 10 before using this feature. Once you get the hang of it, you can use it on

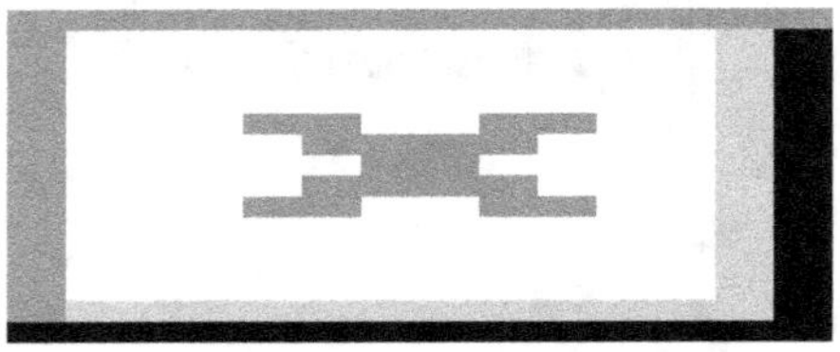

either your iPhone 8 or your iPad.

Multilingual Typing

iOS 10 makes it easy to type in multiple languages at the same time. Before configuring your international keyboard, visit Settings > General > Dictionary. You can then add the languages you wish to add. Combined with configuring your international keyboards, this setting makes multilingual typing on iOS 10 a breeze.

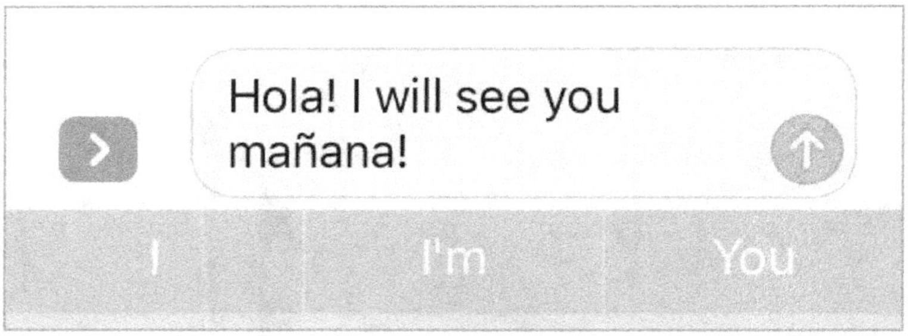

Screenshot 6: Multilingual Typing

Configuring International Keyboards

If you find yourself typing in a different language fairly often, you may want to set up international keyboards. To set up international keyboards, visit Settings > General >

Keyboard > Keyboards (for more about Settings, check out Part 4). You can then add an appropriate international keyboard by tapping Add New Keyboard. As an example, iPhone has great support for Chinese text entry – choose from pinyin, stroke, zhuyin, and handwriting, where you actually sketch out the character yourself.

When you enable another keyboard, the smiley emoji key will change to a globe icon. To use international keyboards, tap the Globe key to cycle through your keyboard choices.

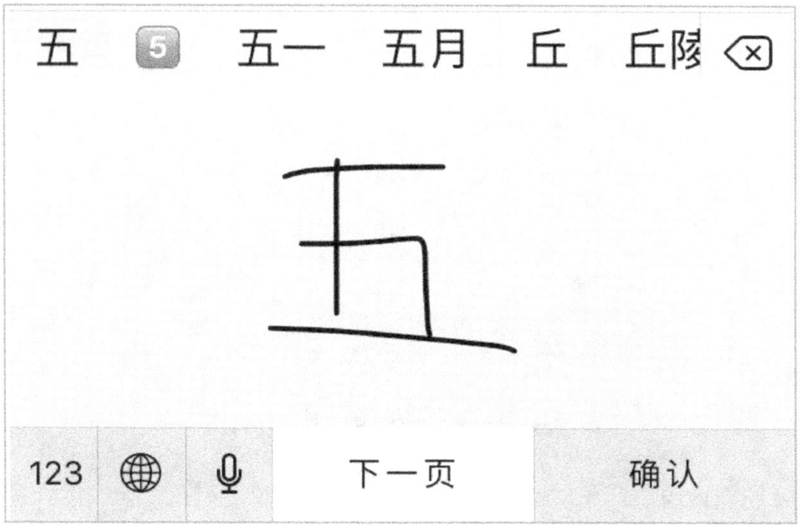

Screenshot 7: The iPhone's Chinese Handwriting Input Keyboard

QuickType: Autocorrect and Predictive Text

Your iPhone 8 is loaded with features to help prevent slip-ups, including Apple's battle-tested autocorrect feature, which guards against common typos. In iOS 8, Apple introduced a predictive text feature that predicts what words you're most likely to type, and its accuracy is even better in iOS 10. Three choices appear just above the keyboard – the entry as typed, plus two best guesses. Predictive text is somewhat context-specific, too. It learns your speech patterns as you email your boss or text your best friend, and it will serve up appropriate suggestions based on who you're messaging or emailing. Of course, if it bothers you, you can turn it off by visiting Settings > General > Keyboards and turning off predictive text by sliding the green slider to the left (for more on Settings, check out Part 4).

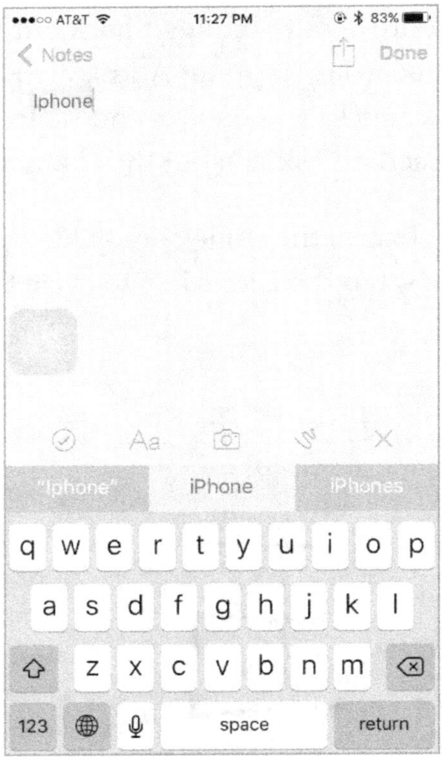

Screenshot 8: Predictive Text

Third Party Keyboards

Like its predecessor iOS 9, iOS 10 allows third party keyboards. If you've been using the Swype keyboard on an Android device – rejoice! It's available in the App Store!

1.6 Setting Up Your New iPhone

Setting up a new iPhone is a breeze, thanks to iPhone's built-in Setup Assistant. iPhone will walk you through the initial setup step by step, and we'll give you the details as you go.

If you haven't done so already, press and hold the sleep/wake button to turn on your new iPhone. Look at the bottom of the screen. You'll see an arrow and the message "slide to set up," which will cycle through several languages. Take your finger, touch the arrow, and swipe your finger across the screen.

Wait while your iPhone is activated.

Next, you'll be prompted to select your preferred language and your country or region. Select by tapping, and use the Back text in the upper left corner if you make a mistake or change your mind about anything while working through the setup process.

Now, connect your iPhone to a wireless network, if one is available. You may need to enter a password. If you don't have a wireless connection, you can connect using cellular data (3G or 4G LTE), though remember that using a wireless network won't affect your data plan with your wireless carrier, while using 3G may count toward data plan limits.

At this point, you may need to activate your iPhone through your carrier.

Now you'll decide whether or not to enable Location Services. Location Services add all kinds of fun and convenience to many apps - for example, Maps can find your current location and use it as a starting point for route directions, and Camera can automatically tag your photos with your location. However, this also means that you're allowing your device to read and transmit your physical location, and it can shorten your battery life considerably. You'll need to decide for yourself how you feel about this, though you'll be able to change your mind later.

Tip: the blue arrow icon displayed on the Location Services screen will show up in many location-based apps. Tapping it will usually reveal your current location on a map or information relevant to your current location.

Next, you'll be prompted to set up your Touch ID. You can skip this if you want to, but we strongly recommend taking advantage of the security and convenience this feature offers, especially with the third-generation Touch ID sensor on the iPhone 8. Touch ID will allow you to unlock your phone by simply touching the Home button. You can also make purchases on iTunes or the App Store without entering your Apple ID. To set up your Touch ID, repeatedly touch the Home button until your phone is able to read a complete print. This may take several tries, but don't worry - we've found it to be remarkably adept at reading your print after you complete this step!

Screenshot 9: Configuring Touch ID

Next, you'll be prompted to enter a passcode. If you're using Touch ID, this will be required so that you can get into your phone even if the Touch ID sensor malfunctions. Even if you've chosen not to use Touch ID, entering a passcode still isn't a bad idea. A passcode is a six-digit password that your phone requires every time it wakes up. If that seems like a hassle, though, just tap Don't Add Passcode. You can always change this setting later if you need to.

After you've set up your passcode, decide whether or not to use Touch ID for the App Store and iTunes.

Next, you'll have the option to restore from a backup. If you've backed up an older iPhone either in iCloud or in iTunes, you can restore it here. Otherwise, just tap Set up as New iPhone. Note that even if you do have a backed up version and want to start from scratch, it's fine to do so.

Next up is the Apple ID screen. If you already have one, go ahead and sign in. If you don't, take the time to create one now by tapping Create a Free Apple ID. Your Apple ID makes it possible to download apps from the App Store and content from iTunes. Without an Apple ID, you'll find it very difficult to get the most out of your iPhone.

The Apple ID is completely free – just follow the prompts and enter the information requested. Be sure to choose a secure password that you can remember. You'll be using it every time you install a new app or buy a new song or video.

At this point, you'll have the opportunity to set up two-factor authentication, a feature previously added in iOS 9. Adding two-factor authentication is a great way to enhance your security, and in a world full of high-profile hacking scandals, we recommend taking every precaution possible.

Now agree to the Terms and Conditions by tapping Agree, and then tapping Agree one more time in the box that pops up. It's a chore, but it's always a good idea to read through these binding legal agreements!

Wait while your Apple ID is set up.

Now, decide whether you want to use iCloud with your iPhone. We strongly recommend opting in, especially if you have more than one Apple device. However, even if your iPhone is your first foray into the Apple world, you could wind up with other devices or newer models in the future. iCloud will make it much, much easier to transfer your purchased content and your photos, contacts, and other content to new devices.

After your Apple ID is set up and ready to go, you'll have the chance to set up Apple Pay. This feature allows you to use your phone as a wallet. Scan your credit cards and your phone will store them for you in your Wallet app (note that some banks still do not support Apple Pay, and you can find a list of institutions that do at https://support.apple.com/en-us/HT204916).

Next, decide whether or not to use iCloud Keychain. This is a password storage system that keeps your passwords synced between Apple devices. Using it requires an iCloud security code or another device with iCloud Keychain enabled.

Next, here comes Siri! Go ahead and select Use Siri for now. You can always turn him or her (depending on your preference) off later, but even if you're not sure it's necessary, we recommend trying it at least once. The Siri in iOS 10 is smarter and easier to use than ever.

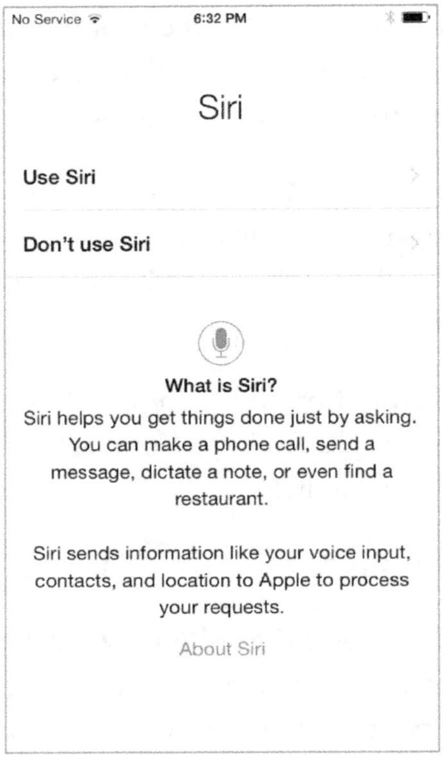

Screenshot 10: Siri

After enabling Siri, decide whether or not to report diagnostic and usage data to Apple. If you're worried about privacy, tap the About Diagnostics and Privacy to learn what information Apple will receive and how it will be used. We recommend taking this stuff seriously.

Finally, decide whether or not you'd like to use a zoomed-in display or not. Due to iPhone 8 and iPhone 8 Plus's increased size and screen resolution, it's possible to fit more apps in a screen. However, if you prefer larger icons, you can choose Zoomed View for a magnified display. It's entirely up to you, and this setting can be changed later.

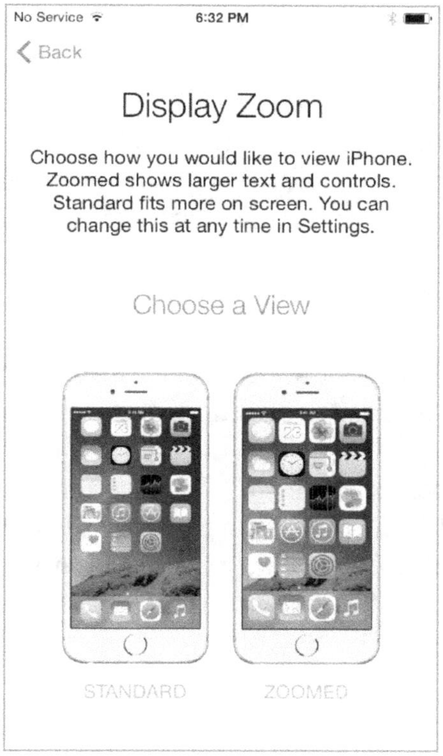

Screenshot 11: Display Zoom Choices

You have now arrived at the final screen of Setup Assistant, so get ready to start using your iPhone! Tap Get Started to view your iPhone's home screen!

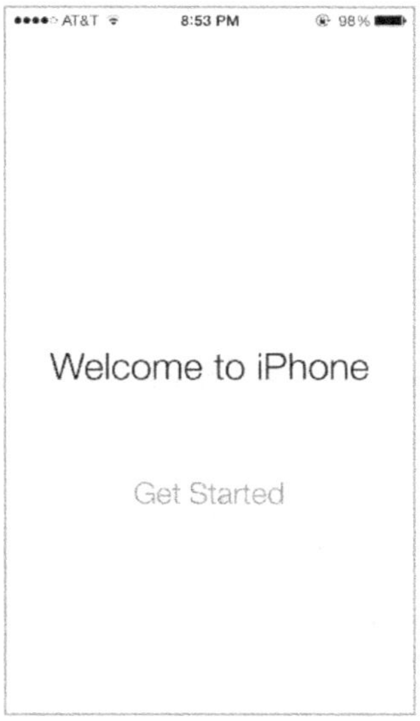

Screenshot 12: Setup Assistant Final Screen

Wirelessly Charging the iPhone 8 and iPhone 8 Plus

It's easy to wirelessly charge your iPhone 8 or iPhone 8 Plus. The process is now more intuitive than ever. With its all-new design, the iPhone 8 has a glass backing that works with Qi chargers which come as accessories. This also makes your phone chargeable in hotels, cafes, cars, airports, and even in furniture. Qi is a universal charging standard created by the Wireless Power Consortium. Mophie and Belkin are just two of the charging mats that are on the market. You can also purchase these through apple.com.

How Do You Charge Wirelessly?

1. Connect your charger to a power source. Use the power adapter that came with your iPhone 8 or iPhone 8 Plus, or another model recommended by the manufacturer.
2. Place the charger on a level surface.
3. Place your iPhone 8 or iPhone 8 Plus on the charger with the display facing up. Be sure to place it in the center of the charger for the most effectiveness.
4. Within a few seconds, your iPhone will naturally start charging.

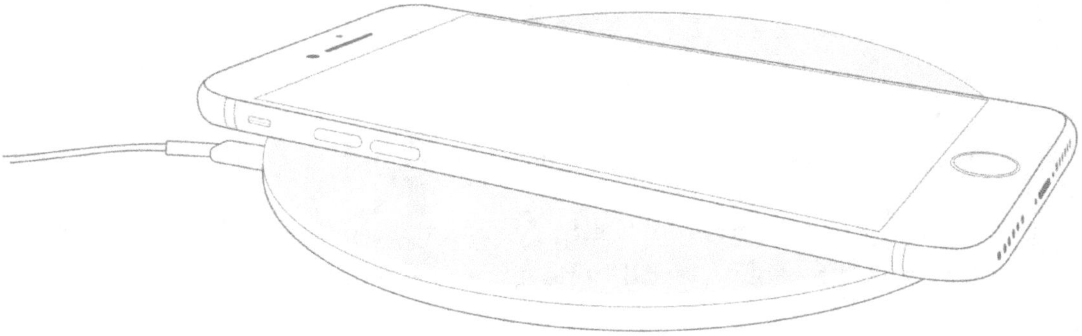

You're going to see  in the status bar.

Wrap Up

In the process of setting up your iPhone, you've already learned and probably mastered some iPhone basics, including tapping, pressing and swiping, and some of the more common navigational elements and where they tend to be located (for example, Back is usually in the top left corner). You've learned where to find all the buttons and hardware on the outside, and learned a little bit about how to navigate the iOS interface. You've also received a preview of some of the things your iPhone can do – Location Services, Siri, iCloud, etc. So take a moment to congratulate yourself. You're well on your way to becoming an expert iPhone user.

We're sure you're champing at the bit to learn how to use the beautiful, layered interface you're now looking at, so read on to find out how to really get started with your iPhone!

Part 2: Getting to Know Your iPhone

Your new iPhone is all set up and ready to use, but where to start? This chapter will introduce you to the basics of the iOS 10 interface. In this chapter, we'll talk about using your home screen, making phone calls, working with apps, and finding other immediately accessible features.

2.1 Home Screen

We'll be referring to your home screen fairly often, and it's what you're looking at right now. The basic look and feel of the home screen hasn't changed much in iOS 10, especially compared to the massive interface redesign that came with iOS 7.

Screenshot 13: iOS 7 (left), iOS 8 (center), iOS 9(right) and iOS 10 (bottom)

You'll return to your home screen again and again to launch apps, adjust settings, and check for updates. Microsoft Windows users may be looking for a start menu or a Documents folder. iOS is a very different operating environment, though. Everything you need is right in front of you… sort of. We'll help you dig a little deeper into your iPhone's features in Parts 3 and 4.

Recent Improvements

iOS 10 gives a great facelift to the lock screen and home screen of your iPhone 8. This fresh look gives users quick access to info and data, and enhancements to Photos will make it easier to find pictures and videos.

Raise to Wake is the new feature that allows an iPhone's lock screen to automatically display when the device is picked up. That means there is no need to even touch a button! From the lock screen, you can respond to messages and receive data from apps without needing to unlock your device. 3D Touch capabilities are what control this kind of freedom.

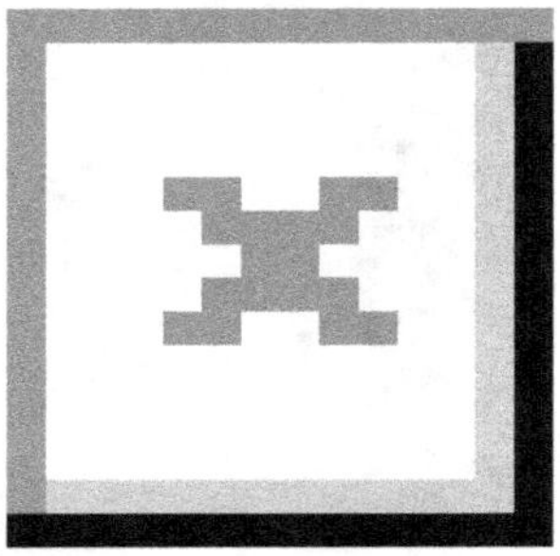

Not only that, but you can quickly clear all notifications from your iPhone 8 lock screen using 3D Touch. The resigned Control Centre from iOS 10 is also something to cheer about. It allows you to swipe to the left for a special area that offers music controls. You can also slide right on the lock screen for quick access to your camera.

iOS 10 also brings us face recognition in the Photos app. This allows you to quickly find your friends in pictures. Object and scene recognition are just on the horizon. This allows you to automatically categorize your photos and videos.

2.2 Making Calls

Presumably you'd like to use your iPhone as a mobile phone. We'll talk about making calls in more detail in 3.1, but for now, here's what you need to know to make your first phone call.

Tap the green Phone icon in the lower left corner of your home screen. This will bring up the iPhone's keypad. Tap in your number and hit the green Call button. To hang up, just tap the red End button at the bottom of the screen. You'll see other options on the call screen, too. If you needed to use the keypad while on a call, just tap the Keypad circle to bring it up. Similarly, you can mute a call or put it on speaker here.

Screenshot 14: Making Calls

Receiving a call is fairly intuitive. When your phone rings, your iPhone will tell you who's calling. If their name is stored in your contacts (more on this later), it'll be displayed. All you have to do is swipe to answer the call. There are some additional options as well – you can ask iPhone to remind you of the call later by tapping Remind Me, or you can respond with a text message. iOS 10 includes some handy canned responses, including "can't talk right now…", "I'll call you later," "I'm on my way", and "What's up?" You can also send a custom message if you need to. If you miss a call, iPhone will let you know the next time you wake up your phone. By default, you can respond to a missed call directly from the lock screen.

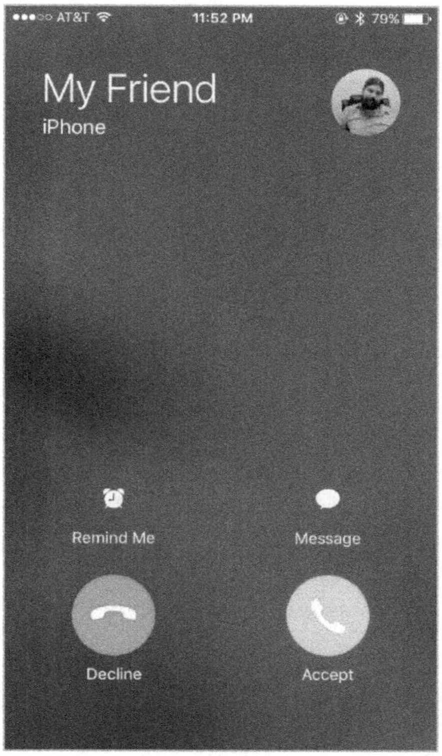

Screenshot 15: Receiving Calls

When a call from an unknown number comes in, iPhone will check other apps like Mail where phone numbers might be found. Using that information, it will make a guess for you and let you know who might be calling.

Tip: New to iOS 10 is the ability for Siri to Announce Calls. You can enable this feature by going to Settings > Phone > Announce Calls. Select Always, Headphones & Car, Headphones Only or Never to choose your preferred way to announce calls.

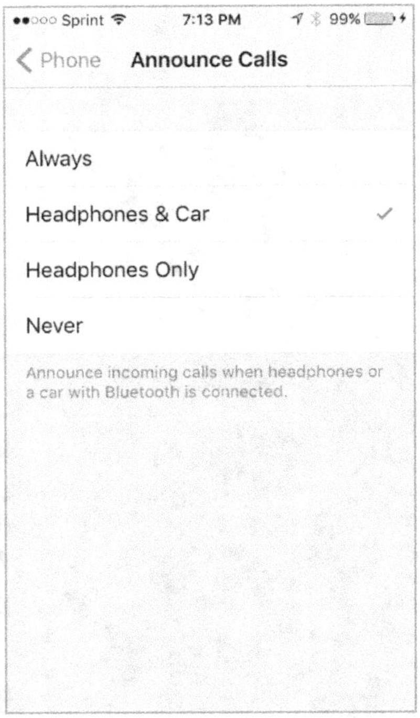

Screenshot 16: Announcing Calls

2.3 Apps

"App" is short for "application." Applications are computer programs, like Microsoft Word, Photoshop, or Solitaire, to name some familiar desktop programs. Now, there are several apps that are included with your iPhone 8, but the true power of iPhone won't be fully evident until you start exploring the App Store (3.5). This is where you can find around 2 million apps for your iPhone. Many are free and most are reasonably priced. If you can't wait to find out more, check out Part 6 for some recommendations.

For now, though, let's learn some of the basics of working with apps. You'll see all of your pre-installed apps on your home screen – these lovely little squares with rounded corners will soon become synonymous with work or play for you.

Opening and Closing Apps

Opening an app is as simple as touching it. Go ahead and open one of your choosing by tapping its icon. To leave the app and return to your home screen, press the Home button.

On the iPhone, returning to your home screen is often all you have to do. However, it's simple to switch between two apps you're working with. Simply double tap the Home button to bring up the multitasking view, which has a stacked design in iOS 10 but still works the same as the Card View of iOS 8. If you're done with an app, use your finger to "flick" it out of the lineup. In iOS 10, your most recent contacts have also been added to the multitasking view.

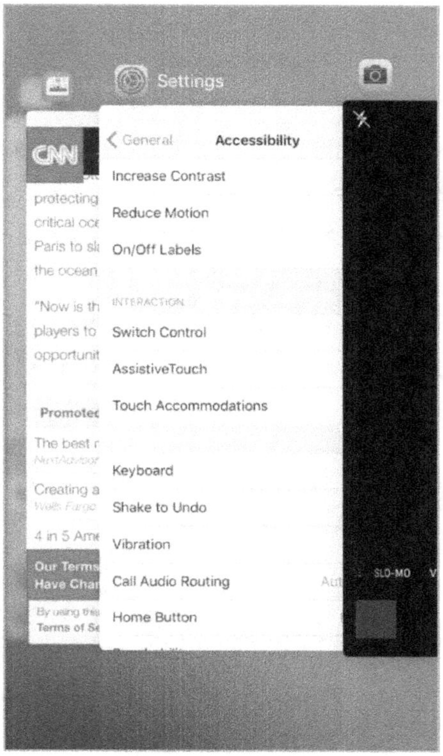

Screenshot 17: Multitasking View

The multitasking view is more than just an aesthetic feature - all iPhone apps can run in the background and refresh themselves without being active. This is great news for a number of situations, but you may notice it has an adverse effect on your battery life. Fortunately, you can adjust your settings if you need to, and we'll show you how in Part 4.3. Apple has also worked hard to mitigate the battery effects of background app refreshing, and iOS 10 claims to be able to add even more battery life through software improvements alone. Plus, iOS 10 is smart - it knows which apps you use the most often, and it pays attention to network strength and time of day. As a result, your iPhone will refresh certain apps more often than others so that you have the information you need and a phone with enough battery power to give it to you.

Tip: If you're an iPad user, you now have the ability to use Split View as a part of the Multitasking View. Being able to use multiple apps at the same time on the iPad is both useful and efficient. You can also view Split View in Safari if your phone is in landscape mode, which is yet another convenient feature. Using Split View is as easy as one-two-three. Simply open an app, then either tap or drag the app divider to start using multiple apps.

Badges and Push Notifications

You'll be notified of new content or events inside your apps by badges – little red circles that appear in the upper right corners of app icons. The specific meaning of a badge varies from app to app – in Mail (Part 3.2), it means you have unread messages. In Facebook, it might mean you have new notifications, invitations, messages or friend requests. Generally, the first time you open them, apps will ask you to allow badges, alerts or notifications. These are called "Push Notifications." While these features can use up your battery pretty quickly, it's an easy way to tell at a glance whether or not there's something that needs checking inside your apps. Most of the time, you'll probably want to turn these on, but you can always adjust your settings later.

Screenshot 18: A Badge on the Mail Icon

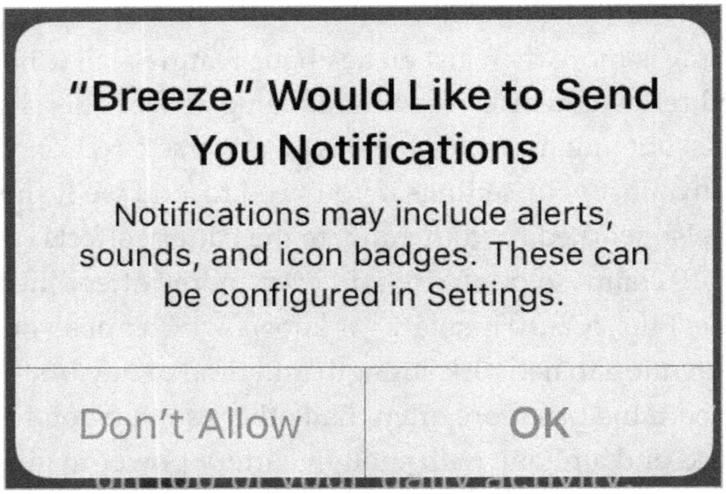

Screenshot 19: The Breeze app requests permission for Push Notifications.

Organizing Your Apps, Deleting Apps, and Creating App Folders

You'll notice that four apps – Phone, Safari, Mail, and Music – are located at the bottom of the screen. This is a good place to keep the four apps you use the most often, because they'll always appear at the bottom of your home screen, even as you swipe from left and right to see other screens full of apps. You don't have to keep these particular four in such a prime location if you don't want to, though. Here's how to rearrange apps.

Take your finger and touch one of your apps. Instead of tapping, hold your finger down for a few seconds. Notice how all of your apps start jiggling? When the apps are jiggling like that, you can touch them without opening them and drag them around your screen. Try it out! Just touch an app and drag your finger to move it. When you've found the perfect spot, lift your finger and the app drops into place. After you've downloaded more apps, you can also drag apps across home screens.

Did we say home screens? Sure! Your iPhone will display up to 11 home screens, and they'll automatically appear as you download apps. Just swipe to the right or to the left to move from home screen to home screen. Take a look at one of our home screens below that's filled with apps we downloaded from the App Store. We're in the process of rearranging, so we've put all these apps in "jiggle mode." There's a difference between these apps and the native iOS 10 apps, though – see the little black X in the upper left corner? By tapping that, we can delete downloaded apps that we don't want to use on our iPhone anymore.

Screenshot 20: Deleting Apps

Unlike previous versions, with iOS 10, you can now delete any of the apps that came pre-installed on your iPhone. This means you can easily remove Notes, Map, Mail, Weather and other apps you aren't using or that you prefer third party apps for. Of course, should you ever change your mind and want an app back, you can re-install by downloading it from the App Store.

Screenshot 21: Deleting Defaulted Apps

If you decide that you prefer not to delete default apps, you can put them out of sight and out of mind by moving them into folders. This is also a good way to increase the number of apps you can install on your eleven home screens, since each folder holds up to twenty apps (disc storage capacity permitting, of course). To create an App Folder, put your apps in "jiggle mode" by touching an app and holding your finger down. Now, drag one app on top of another. This will automatically create a folder. Go ahead and try this out - we can delete the result in a minute.

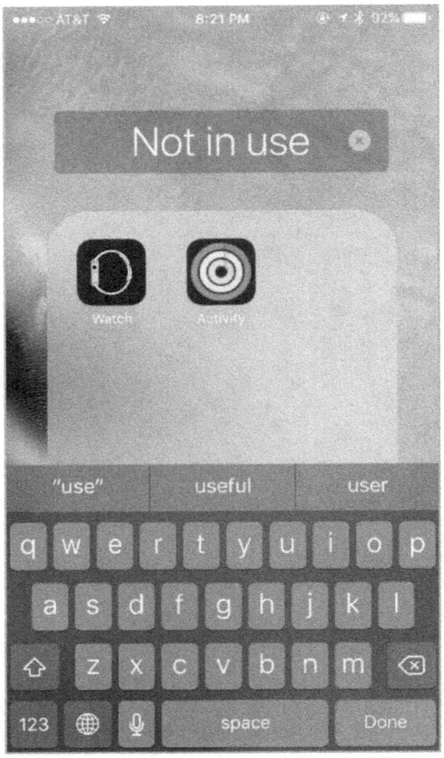

Screenshot 22: Creating App Folders

When you create a folder, you'll be able to edit its name while in "jiggle mode." In Screenshot 21, we've created a folder for Watch and Activity called "Not in use." To delete the folder, just put the folder apps in "jiggle mode" and drag them out of the folder. iPhone doesn't allow empty folders – when a folder is empty, iPhone deletes it automatically.

Back

Introduced in iOS 9, the Back Button is one small change that has a big impact on usability and convenience. When you're in an app, you'll see a tiny Back to [name of the last app you were in] link appear in the top left corner of the screen. For example, if you receive an email notification from Pinterest, you can view the notification in the Pinterest app and then quickly get back to Mail to continue working through your inbox.

2.4 Siri

You'll notice that there is no icon for Siri. If you've enabled Siri, press and hold the Home button. A microphone icon pops up, and Siri will politely ask you what it can help you with. Siri can help you with a lot, too – this feature is a massive feat of computer programming, capable of understanding natural language and delivering human readable/listenable results. Just tap the microphone to ask a question or make a request.

In iOS 10, you can also activate Siri without handling your phone using the "Hey Siri" command. You'll need to enable this by visiting Settings > General > Siri. There, turn on the Allow "Hey Siri" toggle by sliding it to the right. From there, you'll be prompted to speak to your iPhone so that it can calibrate your voice. Just follow the instructions until iPhone tells you that "Hey Siri" is ready. iPhone 8 and 8 Plus will allow "Hey Siri" whether or not your iPhone is plugged in, but any models older than the iPhone 6S will need to be connected to a power source for this to work.

Screenshot 23: Setting Up "Hey Siri"

Siri is a powerful voice-activated system that understands natural language. You can ask her (or him) to adjust settings for you (e.g. "turn on Bluetooth"). She can also search Google, Twitter and Wikipedia for you. With iOS 10, Siri can help you find sports scores, weather, and movie show times. He/she can also send text messages for you, initiate phone calls or FaceTime, add Calendar entries, or give you directions. Siri also includes support for Shazam, meaning she can recognize songs. If you're not sure what's playing on the radio, just ask, "what song is this?" Siri will need to "listen" to the song to analyze it, and she will then give you an answer, along with either the option to buy the song from iTunes or listen to it in your Music app if you already own it.

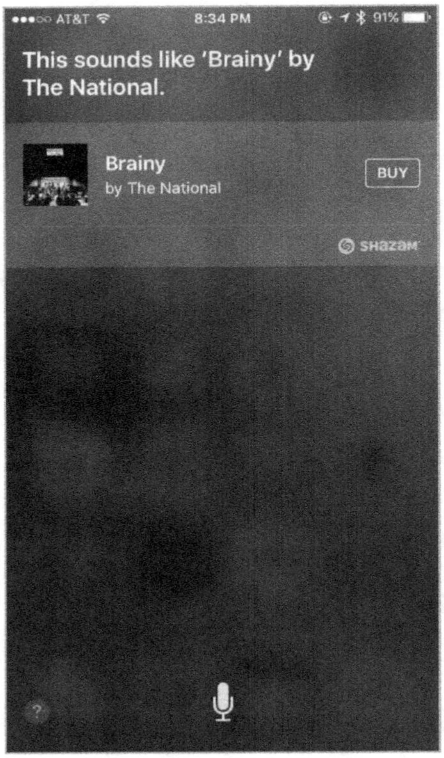

Screenshot 24: Track Recognition in Siri

In iOS 10, Siri has even more useful features, including the ability to work with third party apps. So whether you want to call an Uber or send someone a message in WhatsApp, Siri makes it even easier to do the things you want to do with third party apps using just the sound of your voice. To find out what third party apps work with Siri, check out Siri's new menu listing. To find this visit Settings > Siri > App Support.

To get the hang of Siri, try some of the examples that pop up the first time you open the program. You can always access these later by tapping the little circled "?" in the lower left corner. Siri has added to her repertoire in iOS 10. You can ask context-specific questions ("remind me to read this email later"), and Siri will work with you.

Siri has had some ups and downs, but she reaches all new heights with iOS 10. There have been major changes across the various hardware platforms that support the digital assistant, and you'll reap all these benefits on your iPhone 8. Siri has a new voice that sounds much more natural than the original, and there is a more visual interface that shows suggestions, and even provides follow-ups to your original question.

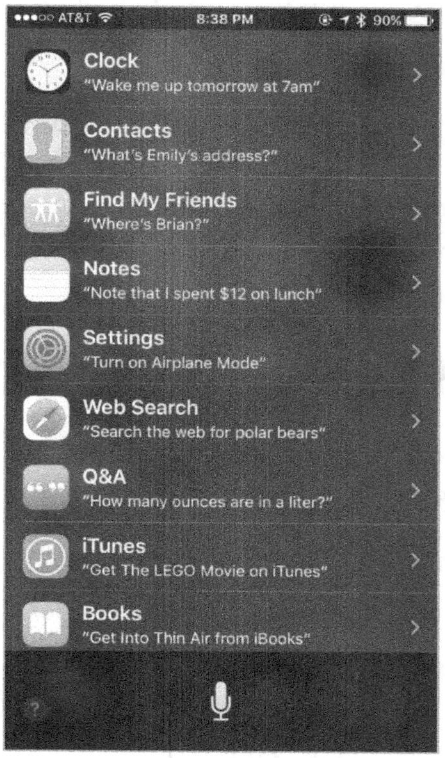

Screenshot 25: Siri Suggestions

2.5 Notifications and Widgets

Notifications can be configured in your Settings, which we'll talk about in Part 4.2. For now, just know that notifications might include calendar events, new email messages, Facebook notifications, reminders, and Twitter notifications. You can access them at any time by swiping down from the top of the screen. To dismiss your notifications, swipe back up. You can access your Notifications Center from inside any app and even when the iPhone is locked, though you can adjust these settings if you want.

As in iOS 9, if you receive a notification of receiving a new text message, you can reply to it from the notification. This means that you can save time and effort by accepting calendar invites, responding to emails, returning text messages and more without ever having to open an app. You can also interact with notifications from your lock screen, unless of course you prefer to turn this feature off.

You can manage notifications interactivity on an app-by-app basis. Simply visit Settings > Notifications and find the app you need to adjust. You may want to do this if you're concerned about privacy, since the phone won't need to be unlocked for someone to respond to messages.

Your Notification Center displays recent and previous notifications. iOS 10 made huge upgrades to the Notification Center by removing today's notifications, which included the weather, stocks, calendar entries, and more. You can now find a separate Today View by swiping right on your home screen or lock screen.

Notification Center includes every notification you've received. You will notice that Notifications look a lot different in iOS 10. Displayed as larger bubbles, the new Notifications take up a bigger portion of your screen, making it easier to notice when a new Notification comes in. Notifications are now much easier to interact with while you're in an app or using other features in iOS 10.

Notifications in iOS 10 are grouped by day, making them simple to manage and clear. In fact, iOS 10 allows you to clear all notifications at the same time by date. To clear all Notifications, use your 3D Touch (if you have an iPhone 6S or later) and click on the x icon at the top right hand side of the screen next to the most recent Notification and all messages will be cleared by the specific selected day.

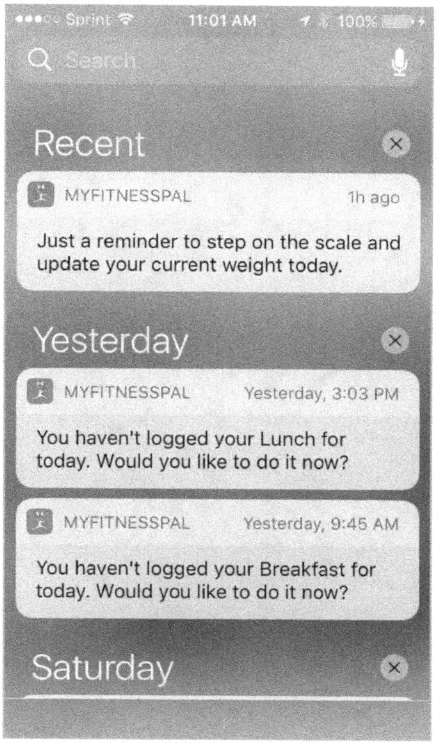

Screenshot 26: Notification Center

Sometimes, you might not want to clear all of your Notifications at one time. No worries. You can do this easily by swiping left on any Notification and selecting Clear. This will remove the single Notification but leave your remaining Notifications in Notification Center.

The Today View, also referred to as the Search Screen, in iOS 10 looks a lot like the previous Notification Center in iOS 9. Today View is also where you can install widgets. Widgets are tiny apps that run straight from the Today View. There's no need to open them or refresh them - they're just there when you need them. By default, your Today View includes the Weather, Calendar and Stocks widgets, but we'll show you how to customize this in 4.2.

Screenshot 27: Today View/Search Screen

2.6 Control Center

Control Center is an easy way to get to the settings and apps you need the most often. Control Center is accessible by swiping up from the bottom of the screen. From here, you can put your phone in Airplane Mode, control Wi-Fi and Bluetooth, set Do Not Disturb mode, and lock the screen's rotation. You can also adjust your screen brightness and access music controls. At the bottom, you'll see icons for a flashlight (using the camera's flash), the alarm clock, the calculator and the camera.

Like Notifications, Control Center is accessible from inside apps and when your phone is locked. You may want to disable this in Settings, depending on your situation. In iOS 10, Control Center looks a little different than in previous iOS versions, but works exactly the same way it always has.

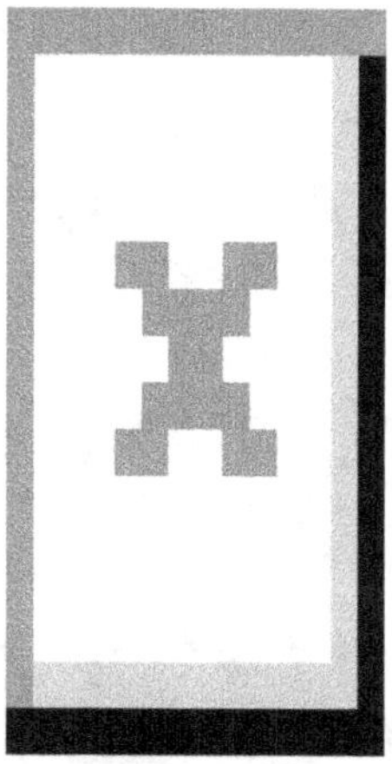

Screenshot 28: Control Center

2.7 Searching Your iPhone (Spotlight)

Searching your phone for contacts, messages, apps, and more is easier than ever in iOS 10, thanks to this proactive assistant feature. The search function in iOS is called Spotlight, and it used to be reachable by swiping to the left on your home screen. Now, just touch anywhere on your home screen (besides app icons) and swipe down to activate Spotlight. This will bring up a search box where you can enter whatever you need to search for. Spotlight will search your music, email, contacts, calendar, podcasts, notes, reminders, messages and more - useful when your content lists start getting too big to scroll through! Spotlight takes search a step further by searching the internet, iTunes, and the App Store, as well as movie times, calculations, sports scores and nearby locations. It's a quick and convenient way to search without fumbling to open Safari or the App Store. In iOS 10, you'll also find a list of Siri's suggested apps.

Swiping right from your home screen will bring up Today View, which includes not only Spotlight but also all of the features found in Today View.

Screenshot 29: Spotlight Search

In iOS 10, you can initiate phone calls, FaceTime, Messages and more from the Search screen. Just tap on a contact to get in touch with him or her.

Tip: See the little magnifying glass in the search field at the top? Any time you see that in other apps on your iPhone, it's usually a search button.

Using Spotlight has never been easier thanks to improvements in iOS 10. You can get to Spotlight from any app by simply swiping down on any app screen. And, of course, you can use Siri to help you with any searches too. Spotlight also keeps track of your recent search history, so chances are if you are looking for something that you've searched for recently, you can quickly and efficiently navigate Spotlight to get your previous search results.

Tip: Not a fan Spotlight keeping your recent search history? You can change this by visiting Settings > General > Spotlight Search and clicking off Siri Suggestions.

2.8 Using AirDrop

AirDrop was introduced in iOS 7, though Apple fans have likely used the Mac OS version on MacBooks and iMacs. In Mac OSX Sierra and Yosemite, you'll finally be able to share between iOS and your Mac using AirDrop.

AirDrop is Apple's file sharing service, and it comes standard on iOS 10 devices. You can activate AirDrop from the Share icon anywhere in iOS 10. If other AirDrop users are nearby, you'll see anything they're sharing in AirDrop, and they can see anything you share.

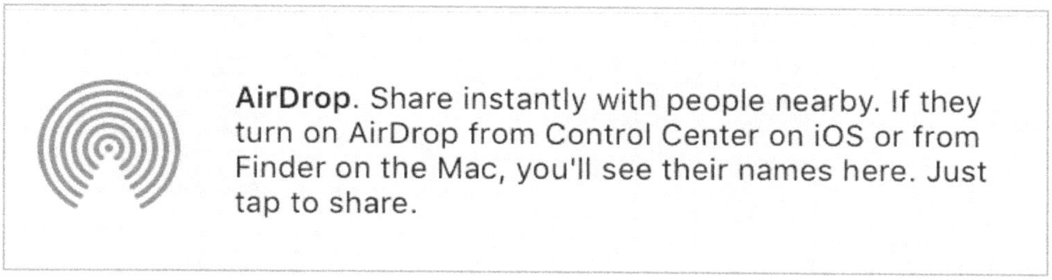

Screenshot 30: AirDrop

You can adjust AirDrop so that it shares with everyone or only with your contacts. It's a very easy way to move content from user to user.

2.9 Proactive Assistant

Proactive assistance is built into iOS 10. It refers to a collection of features that attempt to anticipate your needs by analyzing patterns in your behavior. It powers the new contact and app suggestions on the search page and also helps guide your apps' behavior to minimize your need to enter information or tap through menus. For example, when you plug in your headphones, your iPhone will suggest you start listening to the most recent playlist you were enjoying in the Music app. When you start a new Mail message, your iPhone checks with you to see if you'd like to add contacts that you frequently use. You'll find these suggestions popping up all over iOS 10. It's one of the subtlest improvements of the software, as well as the most innovative.

Wrap Up

Now that you know how to use your home screen, open and close apps, and access Siri, Notifications, and the Control Center, you're ready to start learning more about the pre-installed apps on your iPhone. But before you read further, take a few minutes and experiment. Talk to Siri, get your home screen arranged just the way you like it, and take a peek at some of your apps. You'll be using the information in this chapter over and over again, so it's a good idea to be sure you understand everything!

Part 3: Mastering Your Pre-installed Apps

3.1 Phone

We've already covered the basics of making a phone call on your iPhone in 2.2. Let's go into a little more detail about how to use the Phone feature of your iOS 10 iPhone.

Screenshot 31: Phone App Navigation

Open up your Phone app. There are five main navigation items in Phone. You'll find them in the black bar at the very bottom of the screen. They are Favorites, Recents, Contacts, Keypad, and Voicemail**.** We'll just go straight across from left to right.

Favorites

Your Favorites list gives you easy access to the people you call, message, email or FaceTime most often. You can customize your Favorites using the **+** button in the top right to add names from your Contacts, or you can tap Edit in the top left corner to remove names.

In Favorites, you can make a call by simply tapping a name. If you want to see the full Contact, tap the little blue circled "i" to the right of the name. From here, you'll see that person's full Contact entry, including options to send a message, FaceTime, or share the contact. Be careful, though – hitting the blue arrow can be a little tricky and it's very easy to make accidental calls this way. It's generally a better idea to use the Contacts menu (see below) to access Contact screens!

Recents

Recents gives you a quick look at what's been going on in Phone. You'll see outgoing and incoming calls. Missed calls will appear in red. You'll also see the date of the call. To see the exact time of a call, tap the little blue "i" on the right. Again, though, be careful – tapping the name of the caller will initiate a phone call.

In iOS 10, you'll find your most recent and most frequent contacts in the Siri suggestions section of the Search screen. Just swipe right from the home screen to get there.

Contacts

Contacts stores names, numbers, email addresses, physical addresses, and more. Your contacts live in the Phone app, and also in your Extras folder (3.22). A staggering number of apps can access your contacts (with your permission) – Mail, Maps, Game Center, and Facebook, just to name four.

Inside Phone, you can add and edit your contacts. Contacts can also be synced with outside contact lists (from Exchange or Gmail, for example). iCloud will help you keep all your contacts in sync between all of your iCloud-enabled devices.

Adding and Editing Contacts

To manually add a new contact, click the little + sign in the top right corner of the Contacts display, and then enter the name and information of the contact. You can assign personalized ring tones and text tones for Messages on an individual basis if you like. You can also assign a photo to a contact by tapping the Add Photo circle. This will give you the option to take a photo or choose one from your All Photos album, Photo Stream, or other photo albums you may have set up (3.8).

If you have several numbers for the contact you'd like to add, additional phone number fields will appear after you start typing in the "mobile" field. You can also change the "mobile" label by tapping it. Similarly, you can add multiple email addresses and physical addresses. You can also add notes to your contacts, or several additional fields (Job Title, Birthday, etc.) as needed. You'll need to scroll down a little bit to access all of your Contacts options.

You can also edit existing contacts by finding them in your contact list, tapping their name, and tapping Edit in the top right corner.

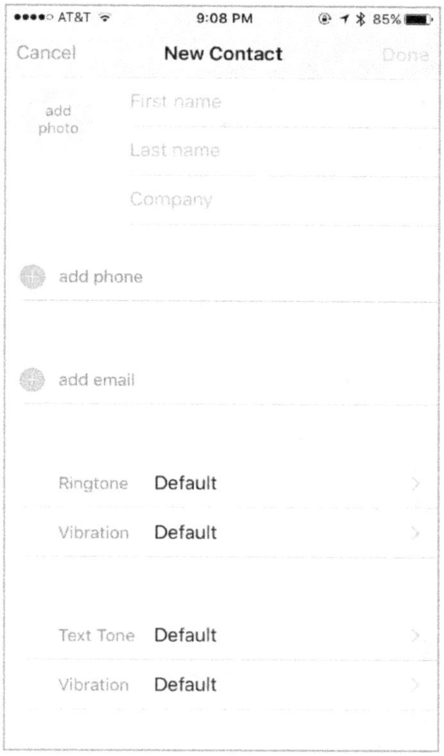

Screenshot 32: Adding a Contact

Using Contacts

You'll use your Phone Contacts list all the time – from each Contacts entry, you can choose to send a message, make a FaceTime call, share the contact, or add the contact to your Favorites list. If you want to make a plain, old-fashioned phone call, just tap the phone number to initiate the call. Of course, you can also do these things through the respective apps. Just start typing a contact's name in Messages, Phone, FaceTime, etc., and the app will access Contacts for you.

Keypad

This is probably the most phone-like feature of your iPhone. It's a numeric keypad for dialing numbers that aren't already listed in your contacts. Just dial the number and press the green Call button to make your call.

If you make a mistake while dialing, use the little x key to the right of Call to delete numbers. If you'd like to add a dialed number to your Contacts, just tap the small plus sign that appears on the left after you start entering a number. This will give you options to add the number to an existing contact, or enter a new contact altogether.

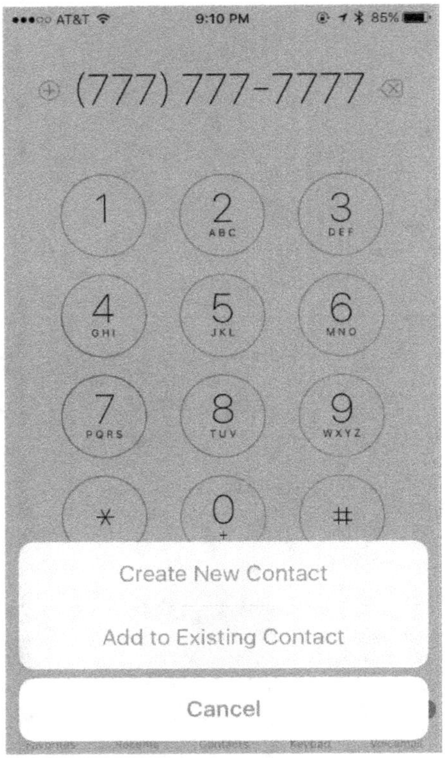

Screenshot 33: Adding a Contact from the Keypad

Voicemail

Finally, voicemail is fairly easy to use – if someone leaves you a voice mail, and you've set it up with your carrier, it will appear in the Voice Mail screen. Tap the message you'd like to listen to. From here, the message will start playing automatically. A menu will appear that you can use to replay the message, call the person back, or delete the message. You can also always edit your voicemail greeting by tapping the text in the top right corner.

Tip: If you have an iPhone 6S or later, you have access to voicemail transcripts. This can be a handy feature. To view voicemail transcripts, simply tap into a voicemail. The display will then show not only the voicemail recording but also a preview of the transcript. This feature is currently in beta and may or may not be supported by your mobile phone carrier. If it is supported, it will automatically display in your Voice Mail message screen in a specific voicemail.

Screenshot 34: Listening to Voice Mail

3.2 Mail

Let's move on to our second app – iOS 10 Mail. If you're already using an email account, a calendar program, or a contacts manager, there's no need to reinvent the wheel on your iPhone. Importing your accounts is easy, and only takes a few taps.

Importing Email Accounts

Tap the Mail icon in the bottom row of apps on your home screen. This will pull up a Welcome screen with a list of common mail services. Choose yours, and follow the prompts.

If your email service includes calendars, contacts, notes, or similar features, you'll have the option to import them next. We strongly recommend importing everything you use regularly!

If you don't have an email address, you can create a free iCloud email account. Just go to either the Mail welcome screen or to Settings > Mail, Contacts and Calendars, and tap iCloud. An alert will pop up with the option to create an @icloud.com email address. It's free, so why not give it a shot?

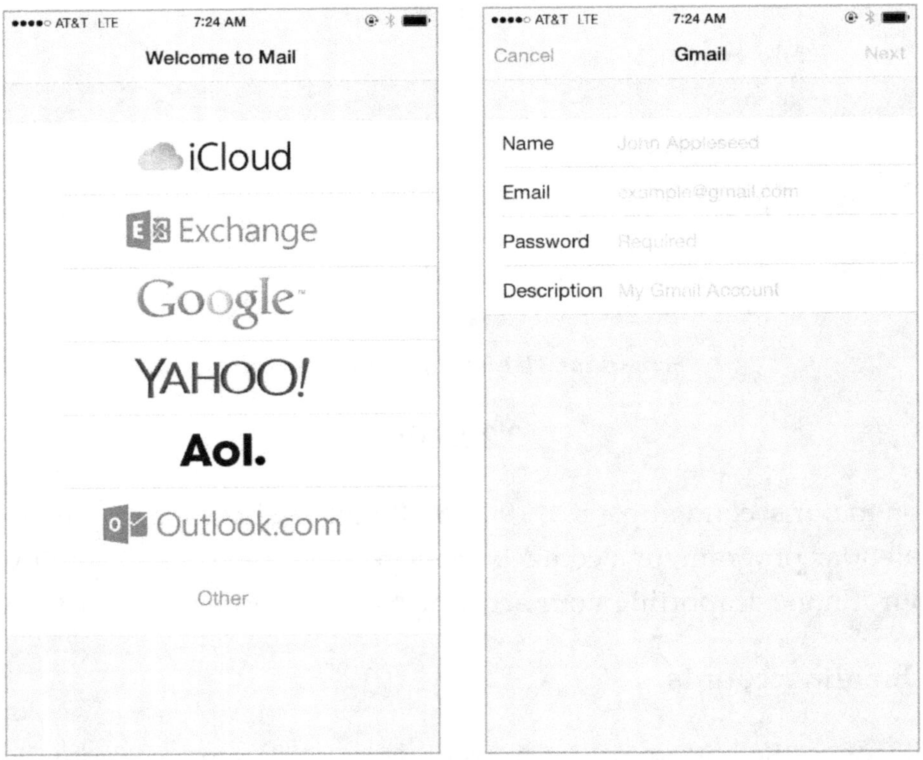

Screenshot 35: Adding a Gmail Account in Mail

If you have more than one email address, visit Settings > Mail, Contacts and Calendars to add additional accounts. We'll walk you through this process in 4.10.

Navigating Mail

Mail is simple to use. To check your email, open the Mail app. Mail will open to the last screen you viewed – the first time you open the app with a new account set up, you should see your inbox. Tap your inbox to see what's new. To read a message, just tap it. To return to your inbox, tap the text in the top left.

If you have folders set up, or you'd like to get to your sent mail or drafts, tap Mailboxes in the top left to get an overview of your mailboxes. From there, if you only have one email account synced in Mail, you should see your folders. If you have more than one account, tap on the account whose folders you'd like to view under Accounts. Then, just tap on the folder you'd like to look at.

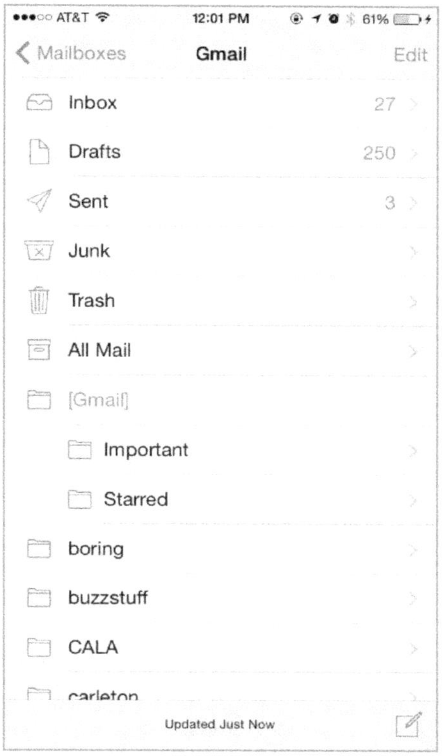

Screenshot 36: Mail Inbox with Folders

iOS 10 also makes it easy to switch between your draft message and your inbox. To "minimize" a new message, swipe down to hide it and reveal your inbox. Just tap the New Message bar to return to your message when you're ready.

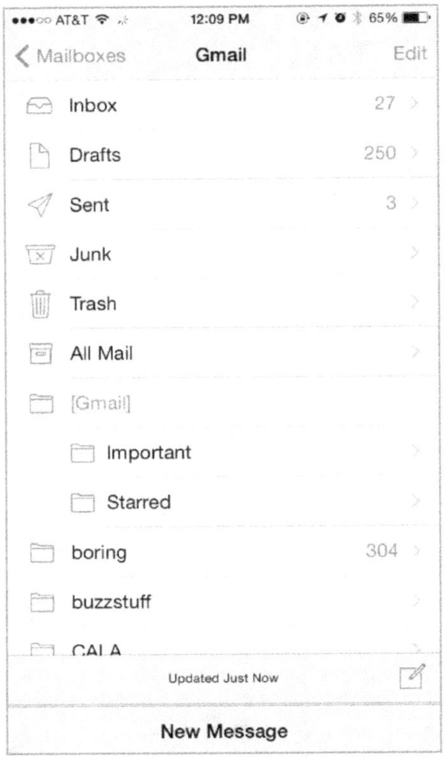

Screenshot 37: A Minimized Draft Message in Mail

Sending Mail

To write a new email message, find the New button. Inside the Mail app, look in the bottom right corner for a square with a pencil in it. This is the iPhone icon for NEW (you'll see it in Messages and other apps as well).

Screenshot 38: The New Icon

Tap it to start drafting an email. It's easy to insert photos or videos from your Photos and Videos apps in Mail. Press and hold anywhere on the screen until the magnifying glass appears. You'll see some editing options. Use the arrow at the left to find the option to "insert photos or videos." If you tap this command, a box will pop up that will let you find and choose a photo or video. Find the picture you want and tap the Choose text in the bottom right. When you're done, just tap send!

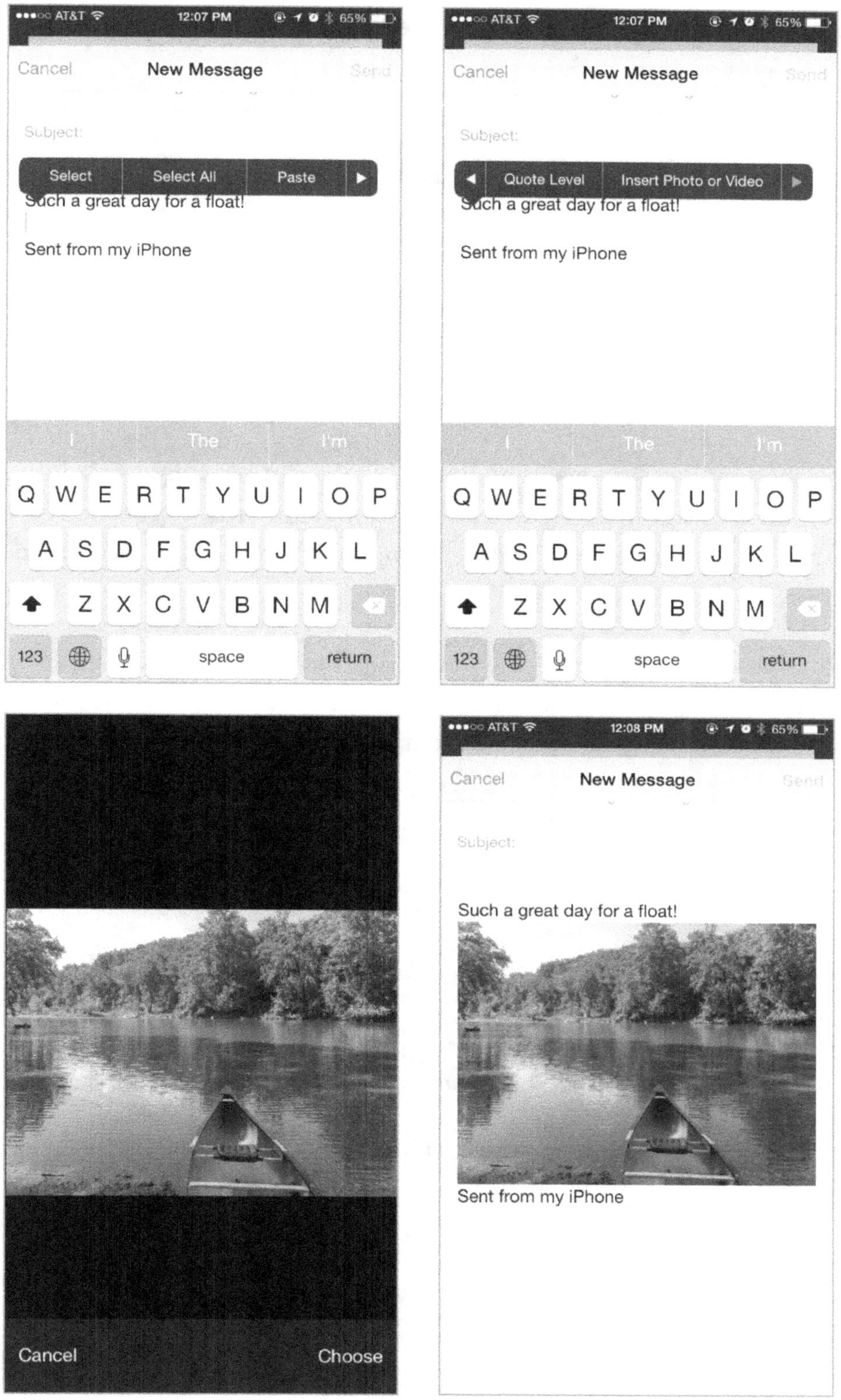

Screenshot 39: Inserting a Photo into an Email Message

Of course, you can also email photos and videos from the Photos app using the Share button. We'll show you how in 3.8.

iOS 10 Mail also includes the ability to add attachments from iCloud Drive or from third party storage systems like Dropbox. This is huge, since it allows you to mail files that may not correspond to an app on your iPhone. If you have a Word document stored in iCloud Drive but don't have an Office 365 subscription, no problem. You'll find the option to add an attachment just after the option to insert a photo, as shown above.

Reading and Responding to Mail

Mail allows rich HTML messages, which means you can see images and photos in the body of the email without needing to download attachments. If you do receive an attachment that needs to open in a different app, just tap the attachment, and select the best application for viewing it.

In the Mail toolbar at the bottom of the Read Message screen, you'll see (from left to right) icons for flagging messages/marking them unread (the little flag icon gives these options when tapped), moving messages to a folder, archiving messages, responding to messages (with options for replying, forwarding and printing messages), and composing a new message.

Screenshot 40: Mail Options from left to right: flag, move to a folder, archive, reply, and compose new message.

In iOS 10, you can also swipe to the right to quickly mark a message as either read or unread.

Screenshot 41: Swipe to Mark as Read

Mail has gotten smarter in iOS 10. When you receive certain kinds of information in your inbox, Mail will give you suggestions, like adding addresses to contact names or adding calendar events for flight times or ticketed events. New to iOS 10, Mail features several easier ways to interact with your email. If you're looking to unsubscribe to unwanted emails, Mail now automatically lists unsubscribe links at the top of each message, so you can unsubscribe with ease. It also includes a quickly accessible filter option at the bottom left corner of your inbox screen.

Screenshot 42: New Filter Option Mail

Multiple Accounts

iPhone makes it pretty simple to manage multiple email accounts. Inside the Mail app, you'll have the option to view all of your mailboxes. These include All Inboxes, VIP, your account inbox(s), and a list of linked accounts. You can get straight to your inboxes, or you can access any folders you may have set up by tapping the appropriate account. Take a look at the screenshot below to see what multiple accounts in Mail look like.

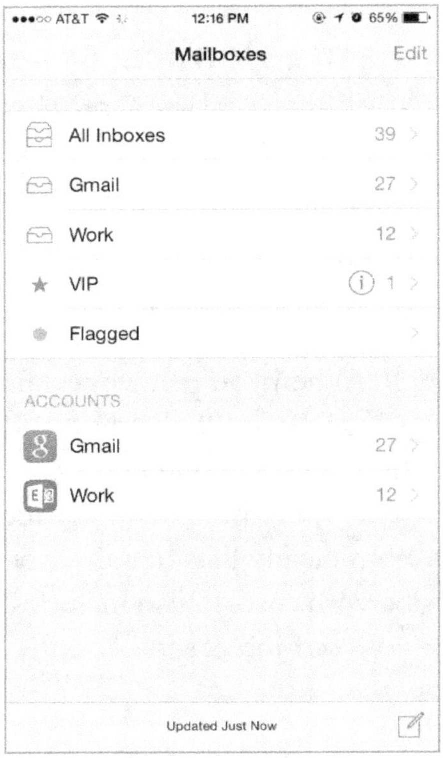

Screenshot 43: Multiple Accounts in Mail

VIP

VIP is a handy feature for those of us who receive too much email. With the VIP feature, you can add your family, close friends, or boss to the VIP list and never miss an email you care about again. VIP emails will trigger banner and lock screen notifications, which are configurable in Settings > Notifications. This is a good way to be sure that you're alerted every time Mom emails you, but not every time that florist company you used once two years ago sends you a promotional email.

To add senders to your VIP list, tap the blue circled "i" next to VIP in the Mailboxes screen. Then tap Add VIP to add new addresses. This will pull up a list of your contacts. You can also tap the Edit button in the top right to delete VIP contacts. Just tap the little red circle with a white line through it next to the offending name, and it's gone.

In iOS 10, you can also create VIP conversation threads. This is a handy way to keep up with an important conversation, even if you don't want to add every single person in it to your VIP list. To mark a message thread as a VIP thread, tap the Flag icon at the bottom of the screen and then tap Notify Me. Whenever a new message is received in the conversation, you'll receive an iPhone notification (configurable in Settings).

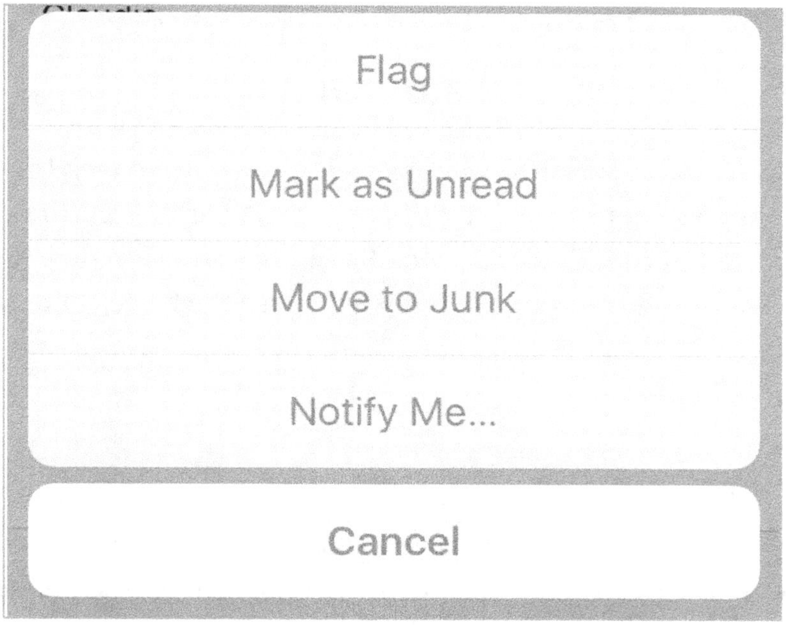

Screenshot 44: Setting Up Notifications for a Mail Thread

Deleting Messages

There are two ways to delete messages in Mail. You can delete a message after you've read it using the "Move to Folder" icon at the bottom. Just tap the icon and select your Trash folder. You can also bulk edit by looking at your inbox, tapping Edit, and deleting multiple messages by tapping the circle next to each message you'd like to delete and then using the Move button at the bottom of the screen to move them to your Trash folder.

You can also swipe to delete messages. Swipe toward the right to pull up the option to trash or archive a message (depending on your mail service), flag the message, or see more options, including reply, forward, mark as unread, move to junk, and move message. If you swipe further to the right, you'll delete the message in one fell swoop (swipe). We had a little bit of trouble with this – we found it very easy and convenient to swipe to delete, but had some difficulty stopping the motion in time to catch the More and Flag options.

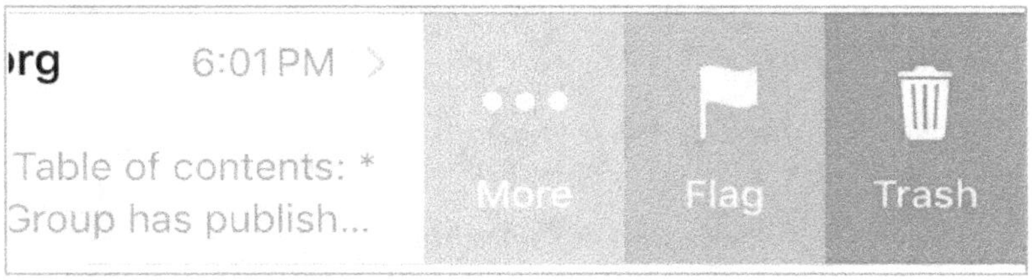

Screenshot 45: Swiping to delete an item.

3.3 Safari

Safari is the iPhone's native web browser (as well as the native web browser on Mac computers and other iOS devices), and it's better than ever in iOS 10. Safari is reasonably similar to Internet Explorer, Mozilla Firefox and Google Chrome, so first-time Safari users shouldn't feel too lost, but we'll cover the basics here to get you started.

Safari Basics

To get around in Safari, you'll most frequently use the search/address bar. Apple has unified the search and address bars so that you can type website URLs and search terms in the same place. This means that you can either type full web addresses, like www.google.com, http://www.minutehelpguides.com/, etc., or if you're not sure what the exact address is or if you're looking for websites about a topic, you can just enter keywords, like you would in a Google search. Safari will suggest the top hit website for you, even if you don't enter a full URL. Try it out a few times to get the hang of using it.

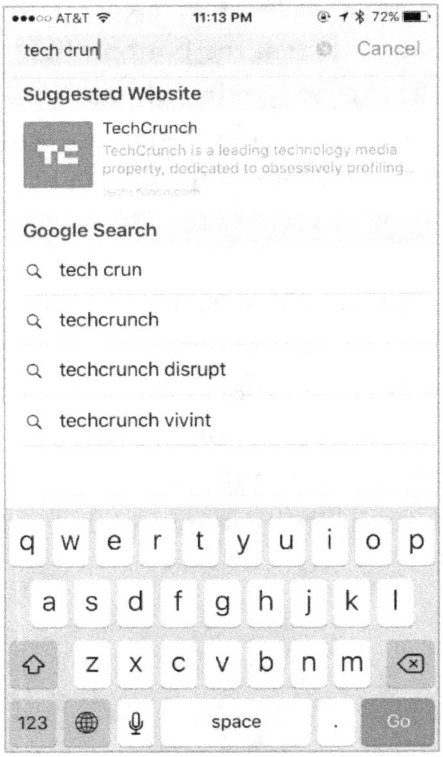

Screenshot 46: Searching in Safari

As you scroll down to read a web page, the search bar will become inactive. This helps conserve screen space for reading, but just scroll upwards if you need to reactivate it.

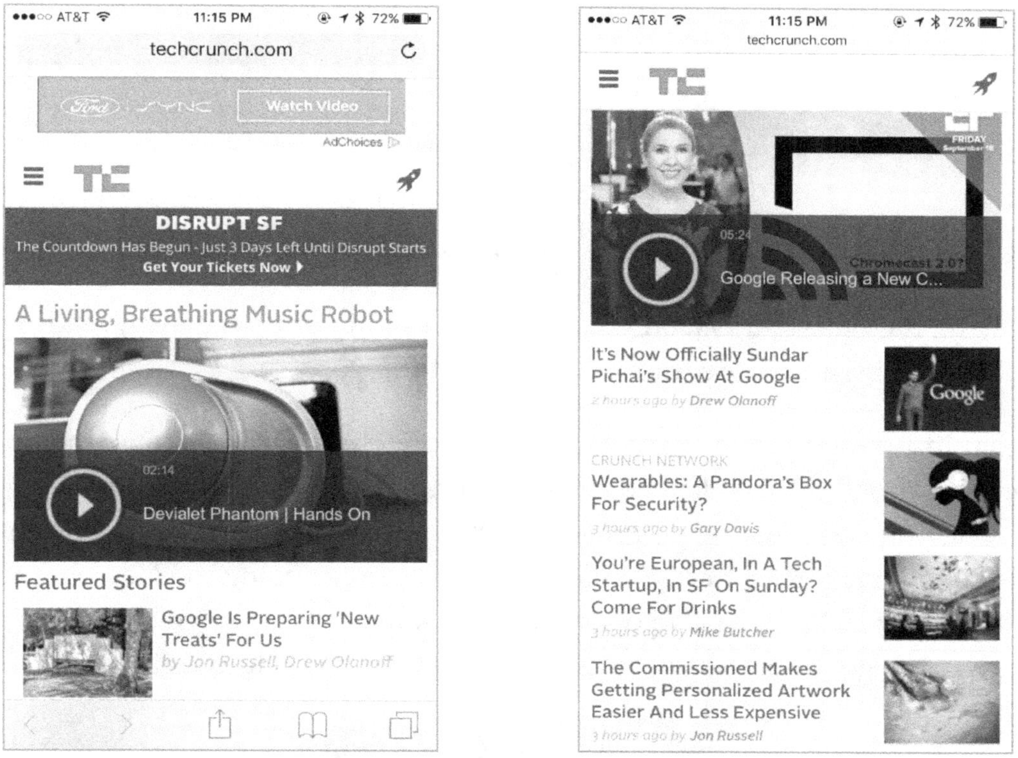

Screenshot 47: Viewing a Web Page in Safari: Active Search Bar (left) and Inactive Search Bar (right)

Settings Tip: You can change the default search engine used by visiting Settings > Safari > Search Engine. Choose from Google, Bing, Yahoo! Baidu (a popular Chinese search engine) and DuckDuckGo.

Safari Tool Bar

The Safari Tool Bar is located at the bottom of the screen in the Safari app. It's only visible when the search bar is active, so swipe upwards if you can't see it. This toolbar includes five very useful icons. They are, from left to right, Back, Forward, Share, Bookmarks (the open book icon), and Open Pages. Back and Forward (the two arrows) let you move back and forward through pages you've visited since you started browsing. The Share button lets you share the page you're currently visiting through Mail, Messages, Twitter, and Facebook. We'll get your own social media accounts set up in 4.12. If you have clumsy fingers, these options will all bring up a popup box that will allow you to compose your share – if you accidentally tap a Share feature, don't worry, it isn't automatically pushed out without your approval! You'll also use the Share icon to bookmark a page, add it to your reading list or home screen, copy content, or print a page.

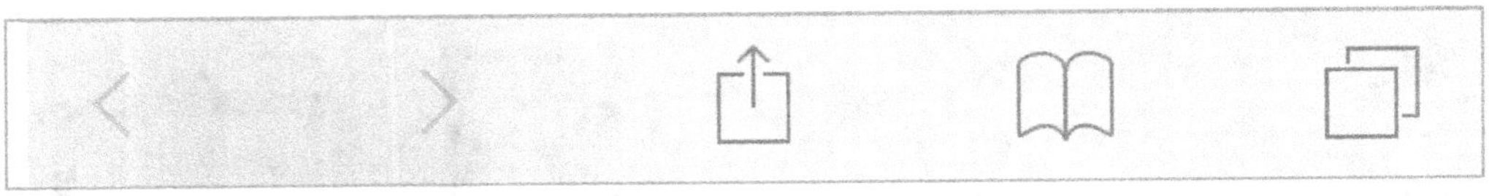

Screenshot 48: Safari Toolbar. From left to right, Back, Forward, Share, Bookmarks, and Open Pages.

Next to Share, the Bookmarks icon gives you access to your bookmarks, reading list, history, iCloud tabs, and more (more on this soon).

Finally, that little square at the very end allows you to navigate between open pages. iOS 10 presents open tabs as stacked cards. You can flick through your open pages and select the one you want just by tapping on it. You can also close pages by tapping the little x in the top left corner, and you can open a new page using the New Page button in the bottom center. You can also open a private tab by tapping Private. When you're done and want to get back to surfing, just tap Done in the bottom right corner.

Screenshot 49: Viewing Open Pages in Safari

If you've enabled iCloud tabs, you'll also see any pages that are open on your other iCloud-enabled devices listed at the bottom of this screen.

Safari Bookmarks

If you find yourself visiting the same websites over and over, think about bookmarking them to save time. A bookmark is a saved link to a web page that is added to a master list of saved links. You may already use bookmarks in other browsers; it's the same general idea in Safari. However, iCloud will sync your bookmark so that you can access it from all of your iOS devices, if you have more than one.

Adding Bookmarks

To add a bookmark in Safari for iPhone, simply visit the page in Safari and tap the Share icon. Then tap Add Bookmark and edit your new bookmark. You can save it in an existing bookmarks folder by tapping location and then tapping your selection. Don't forget to tap Save to save the bookmark!

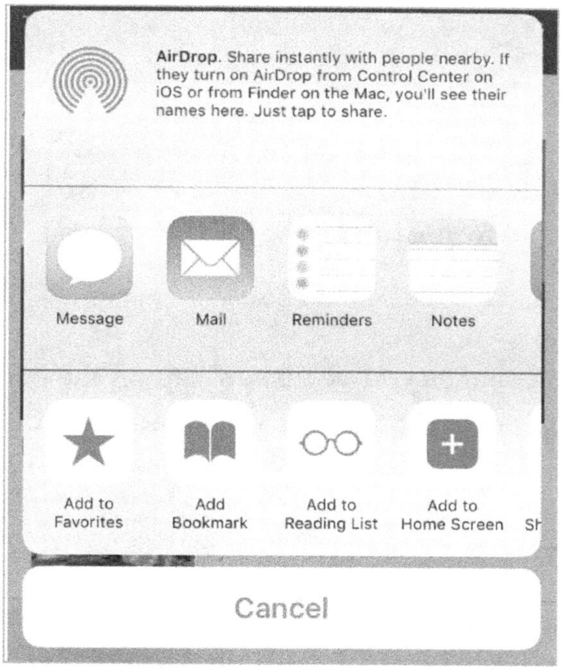

Screenshot 50: Adding a Bookmark Through the Share Icon

Using and Managing Bookmarks

To visit a bookmarked site, touch the Bookmarks icon (the open book icon in the Safari toolbar). To edit your bookmarks and/or put them in folders, touch Edit in the bottom right corner. You can delete bookmarks by tapping the red circle next to the name of the Bookmark you want to delete. You can also add a new folder by tapping New Folder in the bottom left corner.

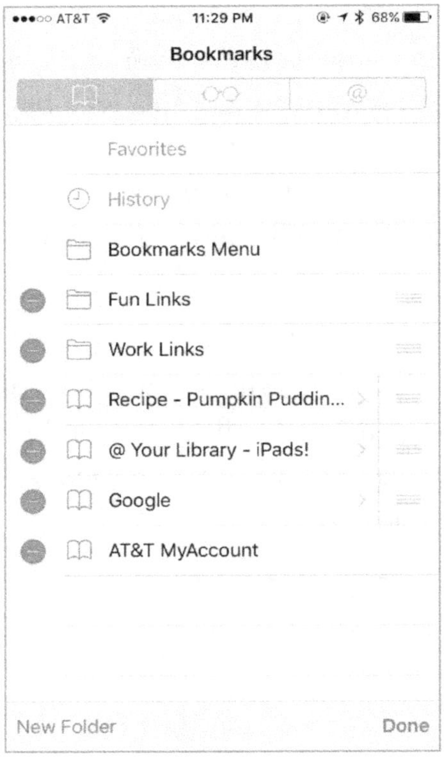

Screenshot 51: Editing Safari Bookmarks

History

To access the history of webpages you've visited, tap on the Bookmarks icon. Then, tap History. History reveals every webpage you've visited since the last time you cleared your History, which you can do in Settings > Safari (see Part 4 for more about Settings).

Reading List

While reading an article in Safari, you can add it to your Reading List. Doing so allows you to come back and read articles at a later time. To add a webpage to your reading list, tap the Share button and then tap Add to Reading List. Like your bookmarks, your reading list is synced across all your iOS devices. Reading List actually saves entire webpages and stores them offline – this means that you can save lengthy articles for later reading, with or without internet access. You can access your Reading List by tapping the Bookmarks icon, and then tapping the reading glasses icon, which represents your Reading List.

Screenshot 52: Safari Reading List

Shared Links and RSS Subscriptions

Safari also includes the ability to see what your Twitter friends are sharing, right from your bookmarks folder. Just tap Bookmarks, and then tap the @ tab to see what content is making the rounds in your Twitter feed. You will need to enable your Twitter account to take advantage of this, and we'll show you how in Part 4.12.

In iOS 10, you can also subscribe to RSS feeds through Shared Links. To do this, visit the site you'd like to subscribe to. Then tap the Bookmarks icon. Tap the @ sign, and then tap subscriptions in the bottom right corner. Tap Add Current Site to subscribe to the active site. This is very useful for blogs and other frequently updated sites you follow!

Content Blocking

The iOS 10 incarnation of Safari includes the ability to install ad-blocking extensions. This is a controversial inclusion that has tech companies panicking about the future of their advertising revenue, but we have a hard time seeing it as anything but a boon for users.

Content blocking requires third party downloads from the App Store. Crystal ($0.99) and Purify ($3.99) are two quality choices available at the time of writing. These "apps" are actually extensions that will live inside Safari. Enable them to block ads, comments, surveys and more.

Safari Autofill

Safari can save form information, including passwords and credit card information for you. When you enter a password, Safari will ask you if you'd like to save it. Just tap Yes. You can also save credit card information for online purchasing. If you're going to use Autofill, be sure to set up Touch ID and/or a secure passcode!

Safari Split View

With iOS 10, iPad users of Safari now have the ability to view two screens side-by-side. This is an excellent multitasking tool and improves on the Split View originally introduced in iOS 9. It's easy to view two screens in Split View. On your iPad, simply drag to one side the browser screen you want to view in Split View. If you want to end the Split View, use the 3D Touch feature to merge the tabs. This feature is currently only available in landscape mode.

3.4 Music, Videos, Podcasts and iTunes

We're going to talk about the Music, Videos, Podcasts and iTunes apps in the same section, since they're highly related. Music, Videos and Podcasts are essentially playback apps for content you purchase (or download for free) in the iTunes Store. To make iTunes Store purchases, you must have an Apple ID set up with associated credit card information.

Understanding Media on the iPhone

The iPhone is a powerful tool for playing video, music, podcasts, and other media. It's important to understand that you'll use the iTunes Store app for purchasing media and the suite of playback apps – Music, Videos and Podcasts – for enjoying that media.

Using iTunes

Launch the iTunes Store using the iTunes icon on your home screen. Look at the bottom of the screen for your main navigation – Music, Movies, TV Shows, Search, and More (More includes Tones, Genius, Purchased, and Downloads). In the Music, Movies and

TV Shows sections of iTunes, you'll see a genre/category browser at the very top. This is a great place to browse for new media. Of course, if you know what you're looking for, you can always tap Search at the bottom and then enter the item you're looking for. Otherwise, tap Genres or Categories to browse.

Screenshot 53: Movies Section of the iTunes Store

Purchasing Content

When you find a song, show, movie or audiobook you'd like to buy, tap the button that displays the price. The button will turn green and display the message, "Buy Song." Tap the button one more time to make the purchase. You will be asked to enter your Apple ID at this point or use Touch ID to verify the purchase. That's all there is to it – your content will download to the appropriate app (Music, Videos or Podcasts) for your enjoyment!

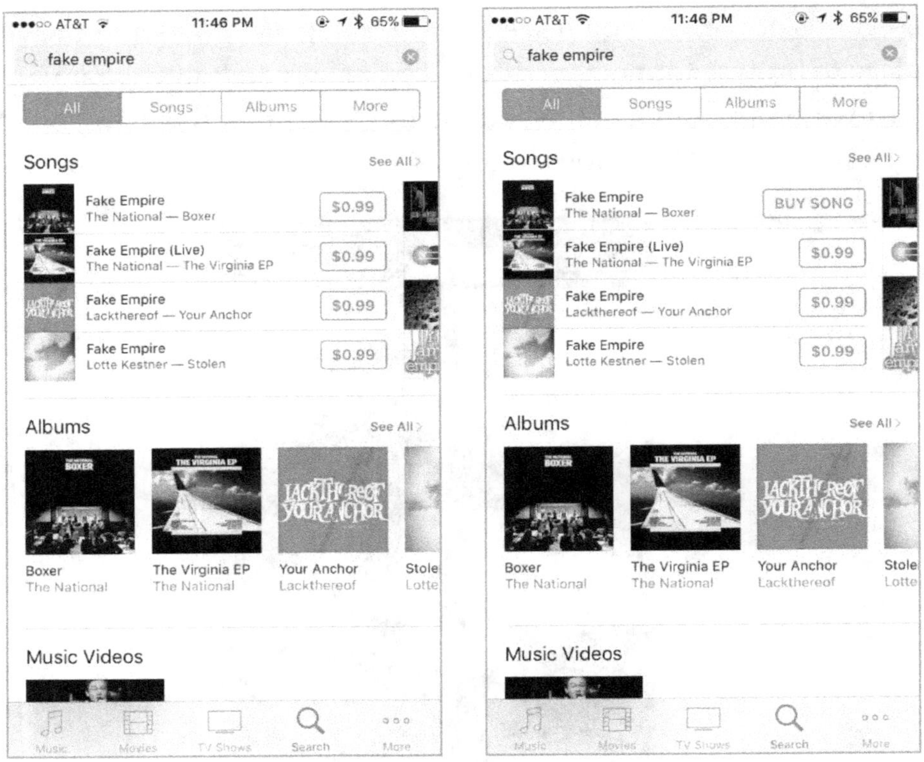

Screenshot 54: Purchasing a Song in iTunes

Note: Movies can often be rented much more cheaply than they can be bought.

Wish List, Radio and Preview History

iPhone will help you keep track of music you think you might be interested in through the iTunes Wish List feature. iTunes will also keep track of each song or movie you preview, each song Siri identifies for you, and each song you listen to in iTunes Radio, which we'll cover shortly!

You can add items to your Wish List using the Share button. Previews and Radio will populate automatically based on your activity. You'll find all of these features using the menu icon in the top right corner of the main Music, Movies or TV Shows screens.

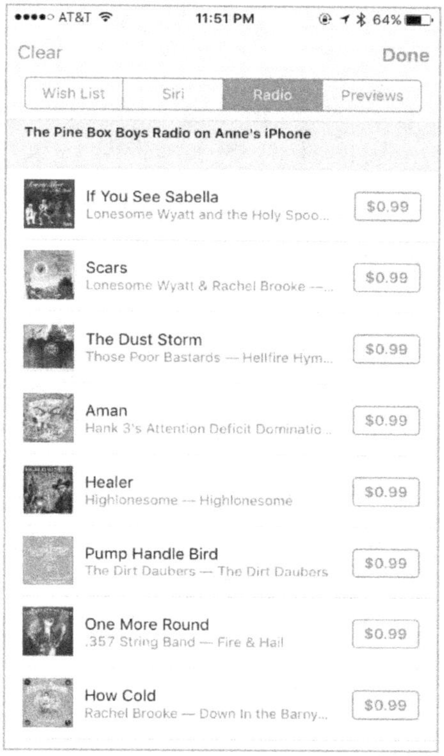

Screenshot 55: Wish List, Siri, Radio and Previews Lists in iTunes

Genius

Genius makes calculated recommendations based on the media you've purchased. It's a nifty feature that can help you discover new stuff. You'll find it under the More Options at the bottom of the screen in each category of iTunes.

Purchased

If you've ever purchased music from iTunes before on your iPhone or any other device, those purchases will show up in the Purchased section of iTunes on your iPhone (located in the More menu by default). Just tap the downward arrow in the iCloud icon next to the songs you want to re-download. You can also download all purchased content if you like. How simple is that?

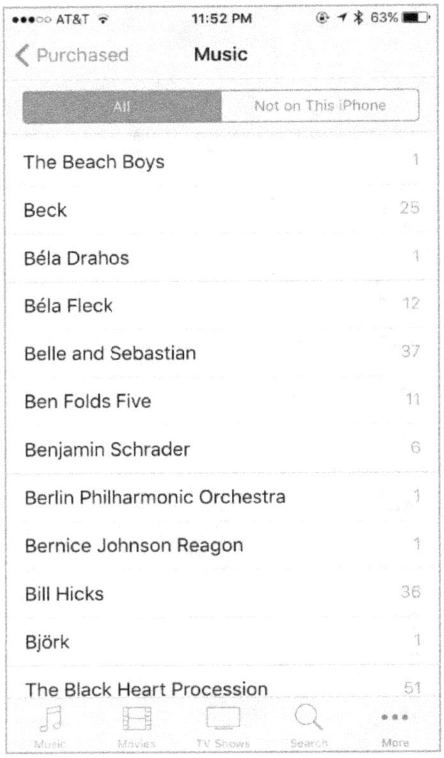

Screenshot 56: Downloading Previously Purchased Music

Music

The Music app has undergone a major redesign with iOS 10. With a clean and streamlined interface, the app offers a more intuitive experience. At the top of the Music app, you can switch between your entire music library, where you'll find your music organized by artist, album, song, genre, composer, or compilation, and your playlists, which include a mix of pre-installed "smart" playlists, like Top 25 Most Played, and your own mixes. In both the library and playlist screen, you'll find the ability to show only music that's available offline.

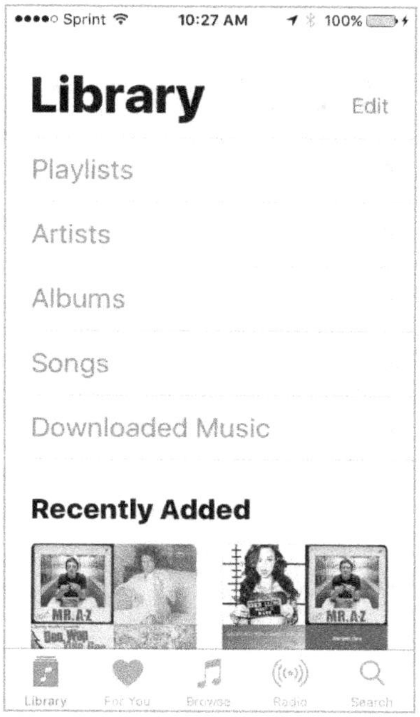

Screenshot 57: Navigating Your Music Library

The Music app features five tabs on the bottom of the screen: Library, For You, Browse, Radio, and Search. The Library is the default display for Music and allows you to easily access your music. A new search tab allows you to search for display lyrics, song titles, and artists. We will explore the For You, Browse, and Radio tabs in the Apple Music section below.

No matter how you choose to use the Music app, iOS 10 makes it simple for you to find the music you want quickly and easily.

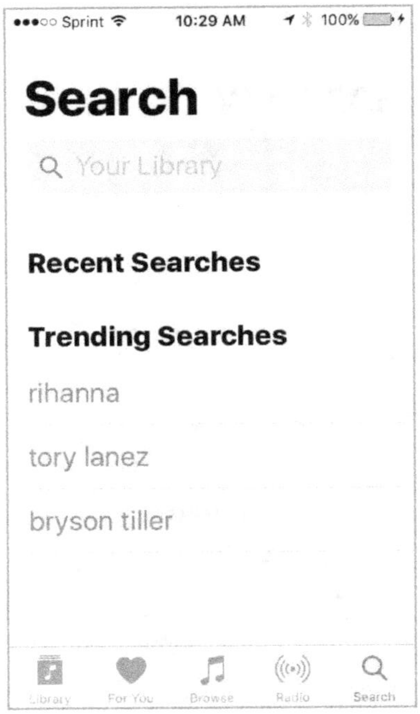

Screenshot 58: Search Tab in Music App

Tip: Music will keep playing even if you lock your screen. You can access Music controls within the app, from the Control Center, and from the lock screen.

Screenshot 59: Playback in the Music App

Music is very intuitive to use, though there are some changes in iOS 10 that take some getting used to. In previous iOS versions of Music, you could easily set your repeating options by tapping the Repeat text in the bottom left corner. In iOS 10, in order to access these options to repeat a song, repeat a playlist, or turn off repeating altogether, you'll need to make one extra tap. To do this tap on the bottom of the Playback Screen. This will bring up additional options, including Up Next, Shuttle, and Repeat. You can also create a Genius playlist based on the song you're listening to or an iTunes Radio station (read on for more information on iTunes Radio!). Shuffle randomizes your playlist order.

Screenshot 60: Up Next, Shuffle, and Repeat in Playback

To return to your full Music library without ending playback, swipe down at the top portion of your screen. This will minimize the Playback Screen. You can return to it at any time by tapping it at the bottom of the Music app screen.

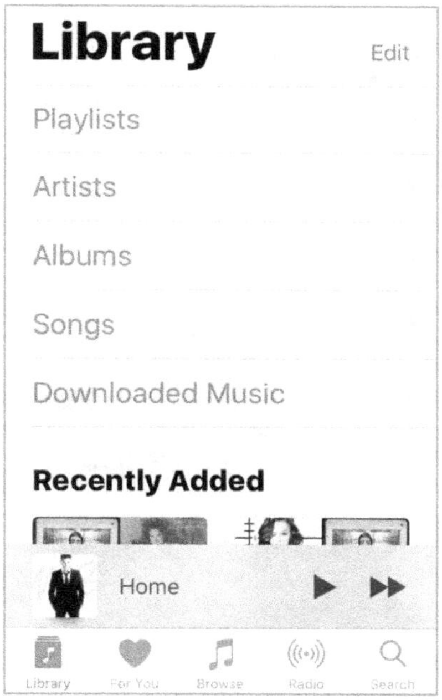

Screenshot 61: Music Library with Active Playback

Apple Music

Apple Music, which lives in the For You and Browse menu items at the bottom of the Music app, is a relatively new service from Apple that gives you the ability to stream the entire iTunes store and receive curated playlists from music experts tailored to your preferences. It costs $9.99 a month, but you can take advantage of the three-month free trial to see if this service is for you before paying for it. It also offers discount subscription pricing for family plans and college students.

If you subscribe to Apple Music, you can utilize For You which displays recommended playlists and albums based on the kinds of music you already have in your Music app or have downloaded on iTunes. Browse lets you look for curated playlists, genres, videos, and more.

iTunes Radio

iTunes Radio, introduced in iOS 7, is a streaming radio service based on your musical preferences. It's very similar to Pandora. To set up a new "station," just tap the plus sign labeled Add New Station (you may need to scroll down to find it). This brings up a list of genres. At the top, you can enter a song or artist you like, and iTunes Radio will build a station based on it.

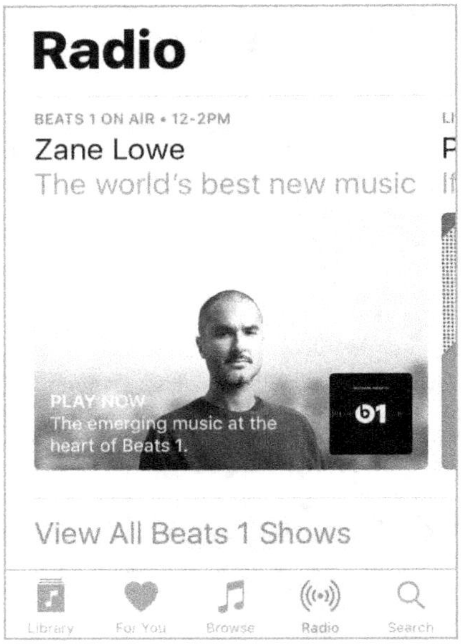

Screenshot 62: iTunes Radio

While you're listening to an iTunes Radio station, you'll have options to purchase songs as you hear them. In previous versions of the iTunes Radio Station, you could use the

Star icon to let iTunes Radio know that you'd either like more similar songs or to never play a song again. iTunes Radio has streamlined this in iOS 10 by using Love or Dislike icons. Clicking on either will achieve the same results from previous versions.

Screenshot 63: Rating a Song in iTunes Radio using Like or Dislike

Tip: iOS 10 has removed the ability in Music and iTunes Radio to easily rate music by Stars. However, you can still rate music in Stars by telling Siri to rate it.

Screenshot 64: Using Siri to Rate a Song

Connect

Music Connect, a feature that allows you to follow artists (and actually it will automatically follow everyone in your library for you), was previously found in iOS 9 as a tab at the bottom of the Music app. It presented a Tumblr-esque feed of pictures, quotes and promotions from your favorite artists. This has been removed as a tab at the bottom of the Music app and can now be found under For You.

Screenshot 65: Music Connect

Videos

Any videos you purchase through iTunes, including movies and TV shows, will be played inside the Video app. Just as in the Music app, with the touch of your fingers you can flick your way through your entire video library. If you have an Apple TV, you can also use AirPlay to stream directly to your Apple TV (the AirPlay icon automatically appears any time an Apple TV is detected on the same Wi-Fi network).

Screenshot 66: Videos

Note: If you use your iPhone to shoot any videos yourself, you'll actually use the Photos app to view them instead of Videos. Confusing, we know.

Podcasts

There's a podcast out there for every interest and taste, and we can't imagine a long car trip without a fully loaded Podcasts library. There are also tons of free podcasts out there for your listening enjoyment.

The new Podcasts app in iOS 10 takes things to a whole new level. What you're getting here is a visual update that makes things clearer. Everything looks more organized, and you'll find it easier to add and listen to podcasts. Also, the new Podcasts app can now recommend podcasts that are geared towards your tastes.

When you open the app, you'll find four tabs: Listen Now, Library, and Browse and Search. You want to start with the Browse tab for finding new content. The Library holds all the podcasts that you've subscribed to. Listen Now houses the latest episodes of your favorites.

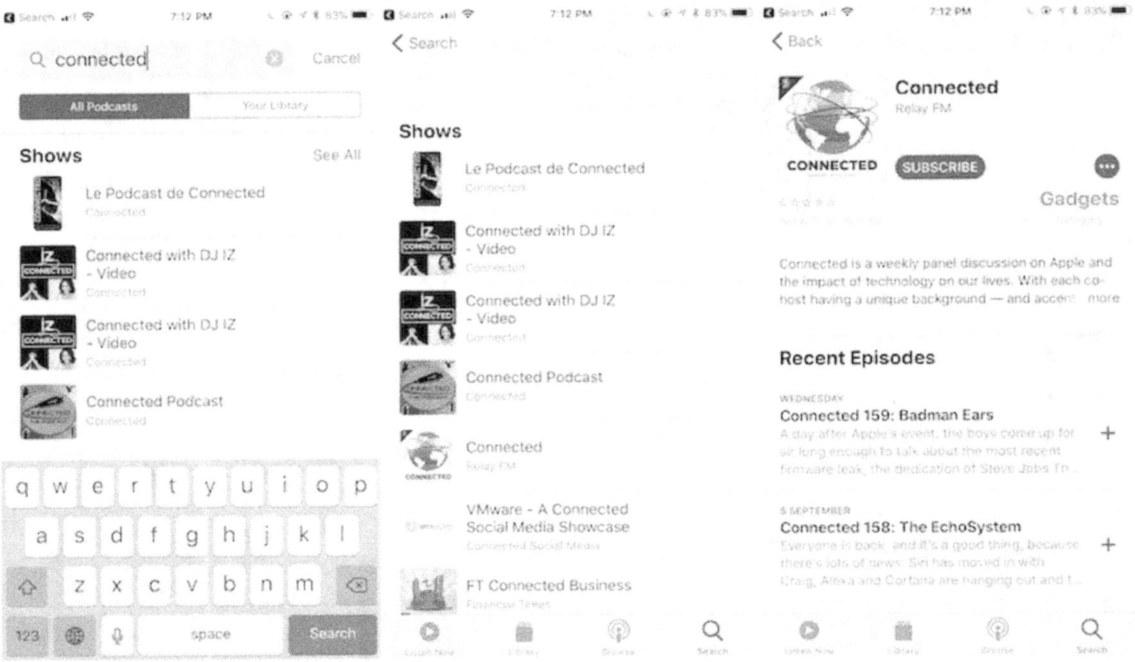

When you're ready to browse for new podcasts, hit the Browse button and a screen will appear that allows you to choose podcasts that you're interested in. When you find something that you like, tap on the Subscribe button, and you're good to go. You can also touch the plus button to add a single episode.

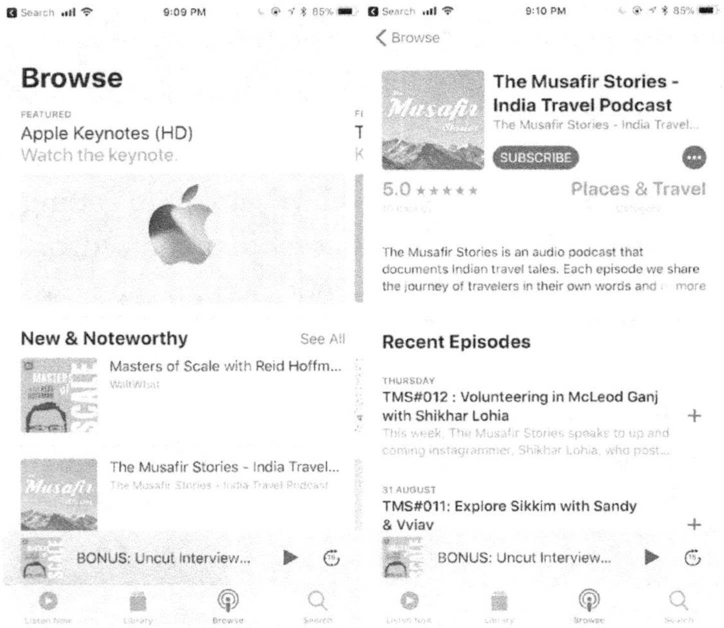

Playing Episodes

To play episodes in the Podcast app, go to the Listen Now section, tap on the episode of choice, and select Play.

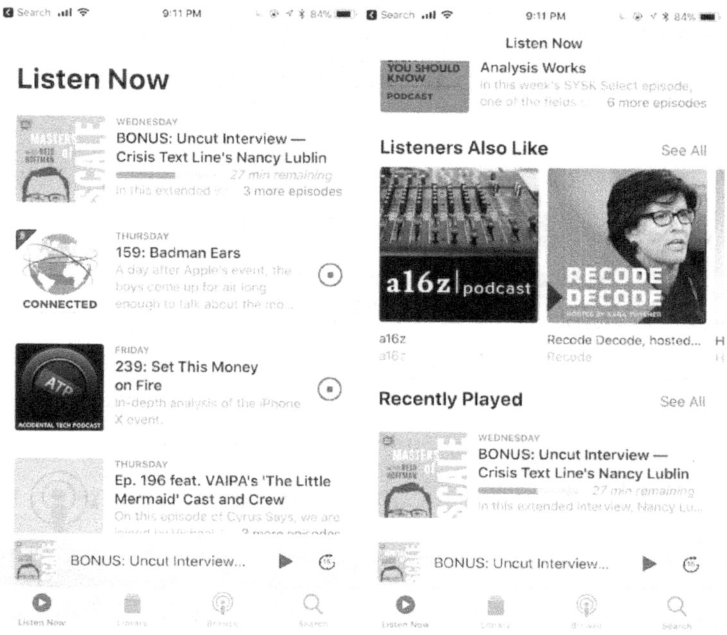

Syncing with iTunes on a Computer

While it's true that you don't have to connect your iPhone to a computer to use it these days, you may very well want to. If you have a large collection of music files on your computer that were not purchased from the iTunes store, you'll want a way to transfer them to your iPhone. The good news is that it's easy to set up wireless syncing between your computer and your iPhone. You'll need to connect your iPhone with a USB cable once to set it up, and then you'll be able to sync over a wireless network happily ever after.

To set this up, you'll need the most recent version of iTunes installed on your computer. Be sure that your iPhone and your computer are using the same network. If both devices aren't on the same wireless network, you will not be able to sync wirelessly.

Connect your iPhone using a USB cable. If iTunes doesn't start automatically, open it up. It should find your iPhone, and you'll be asked to make some decisions about it.

Follow the directions, and when your iTunes and iPhone are talking to each other, find the option under the Summary tab that says "Sync with this iPhone over Wi-Fi" in iTunes on your computer. Check it.

After you've successfully enabled wireless syncing, if iTunes is open on your computer, visit Settings > General > iTunes Wi-Fi Sync on your iPhone and tap Sync Now. Alternatively, you can rest easy knowing that the sync will happen every time you connect your iPhone to a power source while iTunes is running on the computer.

iTunes Match

If you have an *extremely* large music collection, you may want to invest in iTunes Match. This $25 a year service analyzes your computer's iTunes music collection and then matches it with songs in the iTunes Store. If you've got iTunes Match, you can stream your entire music collection, including files that you ripped from CDs back in the dark ages, on all of your iOS devices, up to 25,000 songs (songs purchased through iTunes don't count toward this total). We've found it to be $25 well spent – we love having *all* of our music available to stream on our iPhone without having to sacrifice all of its storage space!

Once you've subscribed to iTunes Match from your computer, enable it on your iPhone 8 by going to Settings > Music > iTunes Match.

3.5 App Store

To add new apps to your iPhone, you will use the Apple App Store. Let's take a look around by tapping the App Store icon.

Navigating the App Store is similar to using the iTunes Store. The primary navigation links are at the bottom – Featured, Categories, Top Charts, Search and Updates. Categories replaces the Explore screen and features popular categories, all categories, and popular near me. Popular near me allows you to search regionally specific apps by top downloads. Tapping on any specific category will bring up the Menu icon in the top right hand corner. This will take you to your App Store Wish List, just as in iTunes. The Search screen also includes trending searches.

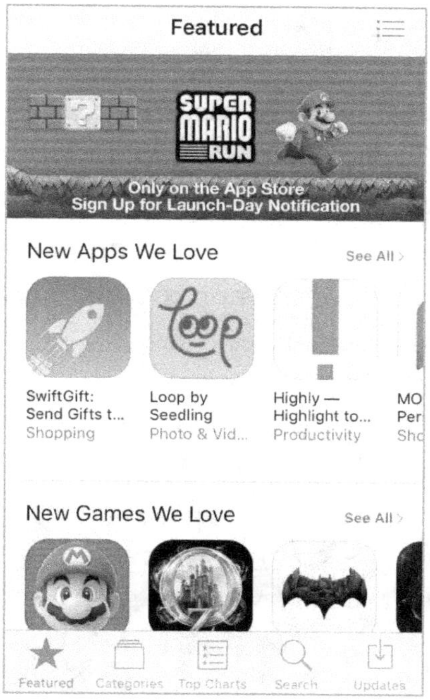

Screenshot 68: The App Store

Other Official Apple Apps

The first time you open the App Store, you'll be asked if you'd like to download several official Apple apps, including the iLife suite (iMovie, GarageBand, iPhoto) and the iWork suite (Pages, Numbers, Keynote). These apps are free for devices purchased after September 4, 2014, and if you have a 64 or 128 GB iPhone, they come pre-installed. Download any of these that look interesting!

Finding Apps

There are a few different ways to find an app in the App Store. If you know what you're looking for, tap Search at the bottom and enter the app's name in the search box. If you're in a more exploratory mood, take a look through the categories. First, go to Categories at the bottom. Once you tap on Categories, you'll notice popular and all categories in a list view. Choose the category you're interested in, and then flip through the apps that come up. Apps are displayed in carousels. You can swipe across to see more, or tap See All for a list view.

If you want to see which apps are the most popular, check out Top Charts on the bottom. This helpfully displays paid and free apps separately – if you're on a budget, there's nothing wrong with perusing the free tab exclusively!

Purchasing and Downloading Apps

To buy an app, just tap the button labeled either FREE or with the app's price. The button will then change to INSTALL. Tap it again. Enter your Apple ID or Touch ID when prompted, then sit back as your app downloads. You can watch your app's download progress with the completing pie chart graphic that begins with the download. You don't have to wait for the app to finish downloading before leaving the App Store or before opening a different app.

Screenshot 69: Installing an App from the App Store

Downloading Free Apps Without a Credit Card

Free apps still require an Apple ID to download. If you want to download free apps, but don't want to set up credit card information with your Apple ID, this is your chance. Find a free app, touch the button that says FREE and then touch the button that says download. From here, follow the prompts to set up your Apple ID, and set the payment method to None.

Downloading Past Purchases

The option to download past purchases is a little hidden in the App Store. Tap Updates at the bottom, and then Purchased to see a list of every app you've ever bought. From here, you can re-download anything you've previously purchased. Note that free apps you've downloaded before will appear here as well as paid ones.

Updating Apps

In iOS 10, apps will update in the background and the App Store will send you a notification when each update is complete. Of course, if you'd prefer to manage your updates manually, you can turn off automatic downloads in Settings > iTunes and App Store. Just switch off the Updates item under Automatic Downloads. This may be a good idea if you're concerned about buggy updates or losing features.

To manually manage your updates, open the App Store and tap Updates at the bottom. You'll see the option to Update All in the top right, or you can update apps individually.

3.6 Messages

This powerhouse of an app handles your text messaging, and then some! In Messages, you can send iMessages to any Apple-using friend or family member, without hurting anyone's carrier-imposed text message limits, and your messages can appear on iPhones, iPads, iPod Touches, or MacBooks running Mountain Lion OS or higher. Of course, iPhone sends regular SMS messages too. In iOS 10, Messages can also send voice recordings and location information, as well as pictures, videos and even animations. You can start a group text conversation with the ability to name conversations, add and delete contacts within a conversation, and mute overactive conversation threads. If you're new to iPhone, you'll get a chance to see some really exciting features. If you're a frequent iPhone user, you'll want to explore this section in-depth because iOS 10 made some pretty major changes to Messages. Read on to learn how to get the most out of what is for many the most heavily-used app on their iPhone.

Tip: Messages lets you know whether or not your Message will be going to a fellow Apple devotee – if your message or the Send button appears in a blue balloon, you're good to go. Green messages will be sent as regular text messages and can count against any text limits your plan entails.

Compose a Message

To write a new message, tap the NEW button in the top right corner. In the To: field, start typing the name of a contact, or enter a phone number if the person isn't saved in your contacts. Type your message in the text entry field and tap Send.

Once you've sent a message, it will display in Conversation View. If you need to see what time the message was sent, swipe to the right to reveal the time of each message.

Add a Picture or Video to a Message

If you'd like to add a photo or a video, tap the little camera button right next to the text field. You'll have the option to take a photo or video or choose an existing one from your Photos app. Find the photo you'd like to use, tap Use, and when you're ready, tap Send to send the message. Though adding a picture or video to a message works the same way it did in previous iOS versions, in iOS 10 it looks a lot different. But don't worry; if you're a messaging pro already, it won't take long for you to adjust to the new look.

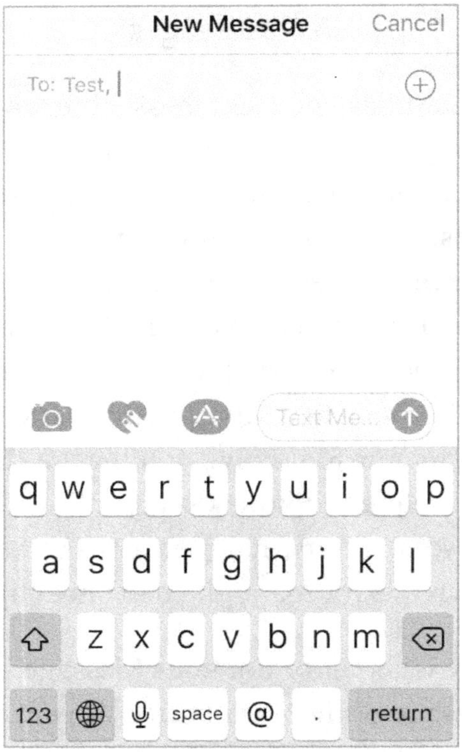

Screenshot 70: iMessage Look in iOS 10

Screenshot 71: iMessage Photo and Camera default screen

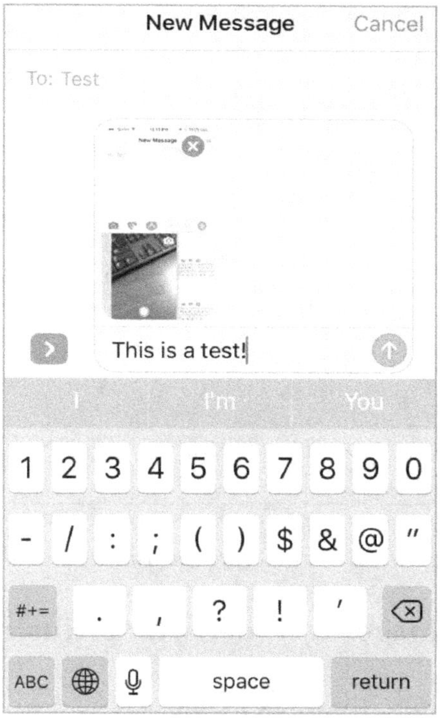

Screenshot 72: Sending an iMessage with a Picture

In iOS 10, you can add more than one picture or video from your Photos at a time – this is a huge time saver for anyone who's used to adding photos one by one! To do this, select photos from the left-to-right scrolling view of your recent pictures that appears when you tap the camera icon. Otherwise, you can tap Photo Library to see your albums.

Send an Audio Recording

You can also add an audio recording to a message by tapping and holding the microphone next to the text message entry field. You'll then have the option to preview the recording, delete it, or send it using the upward-pointing arrow that appears in Recording Mode.

Screenshot 73: Sending an Audio Recording

Send Handwritten Text, Images & Videos, and Music

iOS 10 has added some neat new features to Messages that give you the ability show your personality and be even more social with your friends and family. New to iOS 10 is the ability to share handwritten text messages. To create and send a handwritten message, simply click on the icon in Messages that looks like an A. From there, turn your phone to landscape orientation. Tap in the text field and write your message. Tap Done with your finger and send. It's that easy! Handwritten messages get saved automatically, so if you have a note you want to share more than once, it's easy to use it again without having to re-write it.

Screenshot 74: Handwritten Messages in iMessage

Screenshot 75: Saved Handwritten Messages in iMessage

Want to be even more expressive? iOS 10 gives you the ability to express yourself in so many ways in Messages. Not only can you create beautiful handwritten messages, but you can also send fun images and videos. Find the perfect meme, GIF, or video by searching an easy to access library of images and videos. Like handwritten messages, all you need to do is find the visual image you want to send, tap on it, and tap send.

Screenshot 76: Images and Video Library in iMessage

And if words and images weren't enough, there's an added feature to send audio in Messages. The Music app will share your most recently played songs. Play your favorites and share them with your family and friends.

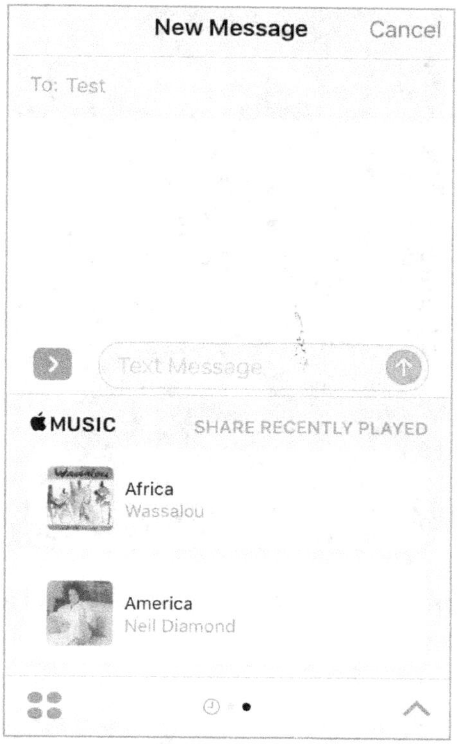

Screenshot 77: Recently Played Music Library in iMessage

Send Digital Touch Messages

In addition to handwritten text, dynamic images and videos, and recently played music, Messages now as the ability for you to send Digital Touch messages. Get creative by sketching, tapping, sending kisses, heartbeats, and more! You can easily handwrite Digital Touch messages, change colors, and even write messages on images and video. To send a Fireball touch the blank Digital Touch screen with one finger, hold for a few seconds, and then release. To send a kiss, touch the blank Digital Touch with two fingers and tap. There's several different variations and fun things to share. With a little bit of practice, you'll be sending Digital Touch messages with ease.

Screenshot 78: Digital Touch in iMessage

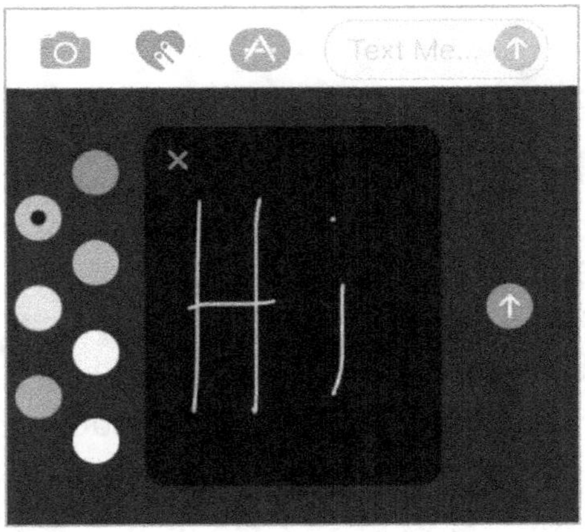

Screenshot 79: Using Digital Touch Sketch in iMessage

Animate Messages

One of the most fun new features in Messages is the ability to create animated messages. Currently available for iPhone 6S or later, this features lets you add animations for a single message or an entire message screen. Adding to the fun is the ability to share personal messages with invisible ink! Messages automatically uses entire message screen effects for certain phrases like balloons for "Happy Birthday" or confetti for "Congratulations." Customize and create your own by either using 3D Touch or by holding on the up arrow to use a bubble effect. For an entire screen message animation, use 3D Touch and swipe left or right to preview different screen effects. Curious how this works and what options are available? Get to practicing!

You'll get more familiar with how this feature works and have some fun at the same time.

Messages with Siri

You can also ask Siri to compose messages for you. Say, "Tell [Name of Friend] hi!" Siri will compose the message and ask if you want to send it. Say "Send" or "Cancel," and let Siri work his/her magic.

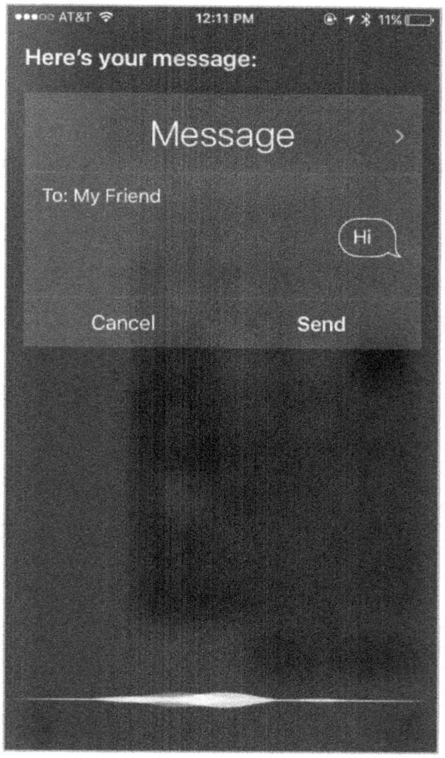

Screenshot 80: Sending a Message with Siri

Send Your Location

It's never been easier to answer the question "where are you?" than it is in iOS 10. To send a Maps snapshot of your current location to someone in Messages, tap Details in the top right corner of the New Message screen. Then tap Send My Current Location. This will send a picture of your location on a map.

You can also tap Share Your Location to allow your conversation partner to see your location for one hour, until the end of the day, or indefinitely – it's up to you.

Group Messages

Starting a group conversation is easy – simply enter multiple contacts in the To: field in the New Messages screen.

Screenshot 81: Starting a New Group Message

Once the conversation is going, though, you can add new contacts to the conversation without having to start a new thread. To do this, tap Details in the top right corner. There, you can add a contact by tapping Add Contact.

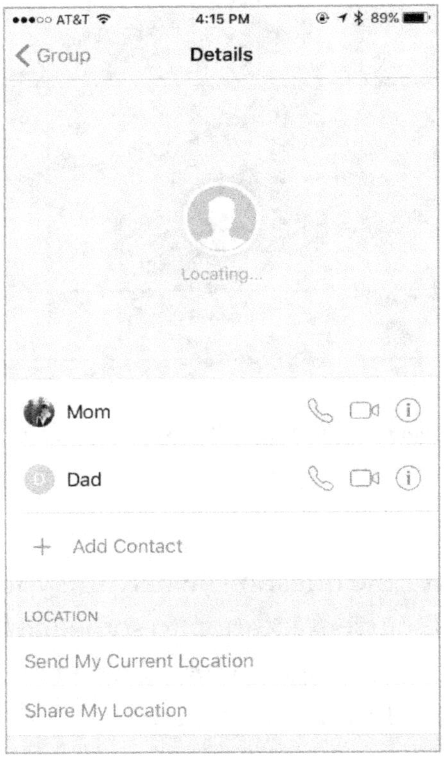

Screenshot 82: Adding Contacts in Group Message Details

If you scroll down further on the Details screen, you'll also find the ability to leave the conversation entirely, or enable Do Not Disturb for that conversation, which will mute notifications. This is great for a large group text session happening while you're trying to finish dinner. At the very bottom, you'll also find every multimedia attachment from the conversation collected in one easy-to-use place – handy for extended family picture sharing!

In iOS 10, you'll see little contact photos for your conversation partners if you've stored them in Contacts, making it easier to tell just who's texting.

iMessage payments

iMessage payments is set to make it easier than ever to give and receive money, right from your iPhone 8. The payments service is built into the iMessage app, allowing you to send and request money with the tap of a button. This service also works with Siri, so you can use your virtual assistant to initiate a transaction. These funds are pulled from your credit or debit card automatically, since this information is in Apple Wallet. When you receive money, it will go into your "Apple Pay Cash" card stored in your Wallet. You can either transfer this money to your bank or leave it on your virtual card. Services such as Venmo and Square Cash are easily integrated with iMessage, allowing users to send money along different platforms. Here's just another way in which iOS 10 is making your life a breeze.

3.7 Calendar

Calendar is an indispensable tool for keeping track of your busy life, and it's even smarter in iOS 10. Like Mail and Contacts, Calendar can be set up to sync with other accounts, like Gmail and Exchange. iCloud will also automatically import any existing calendars you've set up on other iCloud-enabled devices. If you need to sync a Calendar account, you can do so from Settings (see 4.10).

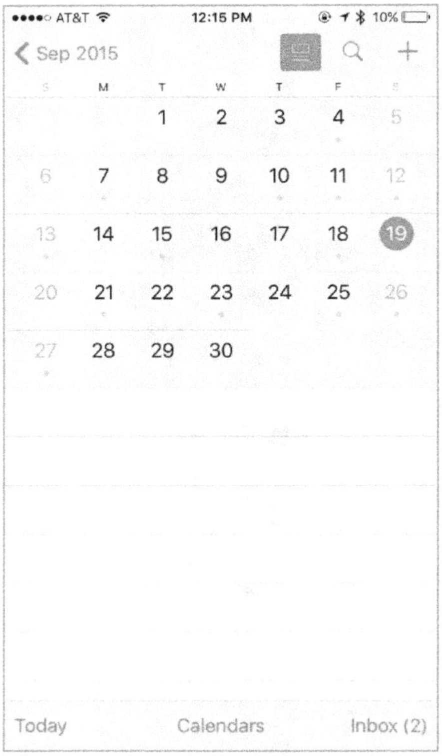

Screenshot 83: Calendar

Calendar defaults to a month view, but you can see everything that's happening on a given day by tapping the day planner icon in the top right corner and then tapping the day. You can tell which days have something scheduled on them at a glance by looking for little dots under each date. The dot indicates scheduled events are present. You can also tap Today at the bottom to view everything happening today.

If you don't use the day planner display mode, tapping a date will bring up a list of everything happening. This can be useful for especially busy days when you need the full display to see everything!

You'll also see Inbox in the lower right corner. This is where all of your calendar invitations will collect for your review and acceptance.

In iOS10, you'll now be able to utilize a found events feature in the Calendar app. The app will suggest events for you based on information found in your Mail and Messages apps. Of course, you can always disable this feature by simply going to Settings > Calendar > Events Found in Apps and turning it off.

Adding Calendar Events

To add a new event to your calendar, tap the + in the top right corner. This brings up the Add Event screen. Here you can enter basic information about your calendar event. You can set repeating events, invite your contacts, set alert preferences, and add availability information, URLs and Notes. You'll see your calendar entries in your notifications, and if you set them to alert you, an alert message will pop up at the designated time.

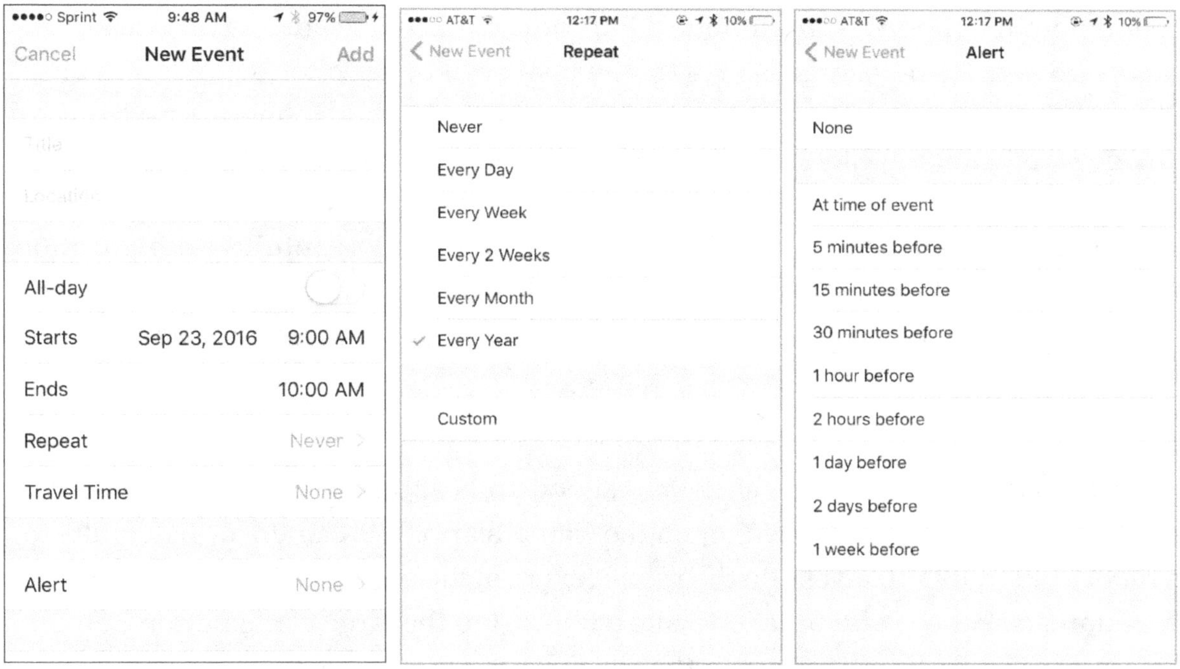

Screenshot 84: Adding a Repeating Calendar Event with an Alert

Calendar, like the rest of your iPhone 8, is smart. When you receive an email with important information, like a flight itinerary, Calendar will add that information as an event. Calendar also now uses Maps for better accuracy in travel time, so it will suggest times to leave based on traffic conditions and transit options. Even better, you can now control when to be alerted based on travel time within the event alerts as shown above.

Managing Multiple Calendars

You can manage multiple calendars by tapping Calendars in the middle of the main Calendar display. This reveals every calendar currently connected to your account. If you want to hide a calendar without deleting it from your phone, tap it to deselect it. Note that if you have enabled Family Sharing, a shared Family calendar will appear. This is a great way to keep track of everyone's dance recitals, conferences, and doctor's appointments. For more on Family Sharing, see 4.14.

3.8 Camera and Photos

The Camera and Photos apps on your iPhone are a match made in heaven, especially with the powerful hardware of the iPhone 8. In addition to 12MP stills, the iPhone 8 series can shoot 4K video, meaning your footage will be crystal-clear and ready for the big screen! Both the iPhone 8 and iPhone 8 Plus now come with cameras that include a f/1.8 aperture and six element lens to help you take even better photos. On top of this, the iPhone 8 Plus camera now includes dual lenses, including a telephoto lens, along with image stabilization. With such impressive hardware in both the iPhone 8 and 8 Plus, there's no reason to own both an iPhone and any other camera but the most advanced SLR models. The Photos app now includes much more intuitive organization and photo editing tools that make using it a joy rather than a headache-inducer. iPhones have always been wonderful camera tools, but this generation is unparalleled.

Using the Camera

Taking a photo is as easy as point, click, and shoot, and capturing video is as easy as lights, iPhone, action. To get started, open the Camera app. The camera app defaults to photo mode, but in iOS 10 just slide the mode text to switch to Time Lapse, Slo-Mo, Video, Square, or Pano (Panorama). To take a photo, tap the large circle button in the bottom center. The flash settings are in the top left – tap the flash symbol to change them. You can also turn HDR on and off at the top center. iOS 10 also includes a timer function, so it's possible to take a hands-free selfie. Just tap the timer and choose a 3 or 10 second delay.

Finally, you can toggle between the front- and backward-facing cameras using the button in the top right. iPhone 8 and 8 Plus include a front Retina Flash, meaning your selfies will have better color and lighting than ever before.

Screenshot 85: Photo Mode in Camera

In iOS 10, you can adjust the focus and brightness of a picture before you take it. Tap on the area of the picture you want to focus on and then adjust the brightness scale that appears to your satisfaction. This is a huge improvement for serious iPhone photographers! You'll also find several built-in Instagram-style filters in the lower right corner.

If you have an 8 series iPhone, you'll be able to take Live Photos. Live Photos capture motion just before and after an image to create a neat *Harry Potter*-esque effect. To view Live Photos, press the screen to engage 3D touch. This will make your photo come to life! Live Photos can be played inside the Photos app, and they can also be used as wallpaper.

Once you've taken your picture, you can open it in Photos using the Photos thumbnail image in the lower left corner of the Camera screen.

Editing Live Photos

Apple introduced Live Photos in 2015, when the iPhone 6s came out. This feature enhances the smartphone's photography, using pictures that move when you perform a 3D Touch on them. iOS 10 makes Live Photos better than ever. Wanna know how to take a live photo? Let's have a look.

Live Photos records what happens 1.5 seconds before and after you take the photo. That means you're not only getting a photo, you're also getting movement and sound.

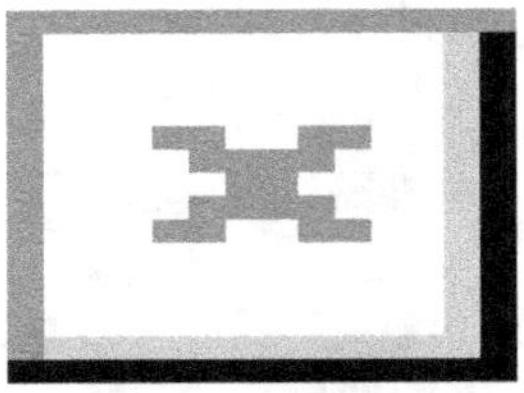

1. Open the Camera app

2. Set your camera to photo mode, and turn Live Photos on

3. Hold the phone very still

4. Tap  .

With your iPhone 8, Live Photos is naturally on by default. If you want to take a still image, tap  and you'll be allowed to turn off Live Photos. If you want Live Photos to always be off, go to Settings > Camera > Preserve Settings.

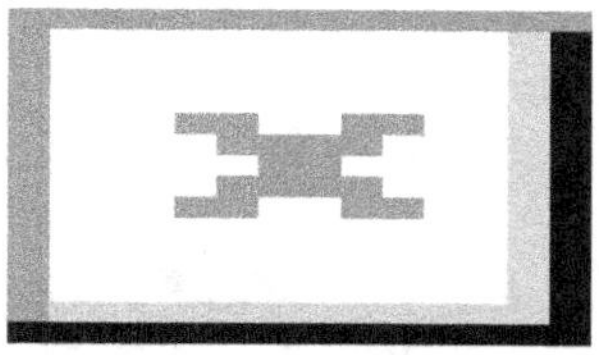

New Portrait modes

Portrait mode is a tool Apple launched with their iPhone 7, and it gets enhancements with iOS 10. The new Portrait mode uses machine learning to isolate the subject's face from its background. This allows for targeted lighting changes that make your photos look more professional. Now, you're able to dim the lighting or brighten a subject's face without affecting other elements of the picture. This is pretty much a photographer's dream.

Using Photos

The Photos app is your one-stop shop for organizing, editing and sharing your iPhone photos and videos. Here you can browse and organize your photos, as well as share them with friends and family.

Navigating Photos

Photos includes four main screens – Photos, Memories, Shared, and Albums. To switch between these views, use the icons at the bottom of the Photos screen.

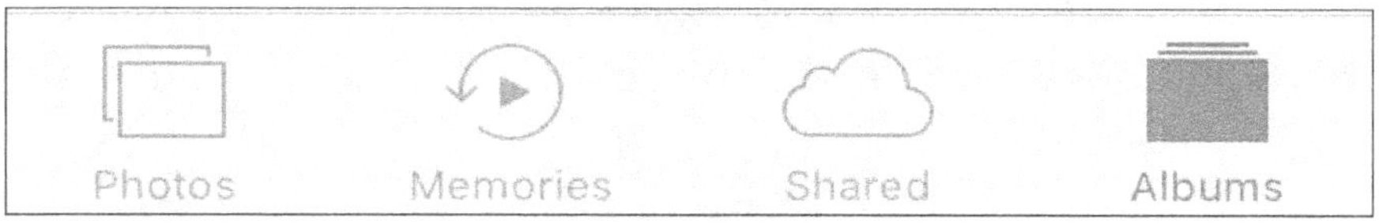

Screenshot 86: Photos Menu

The Photos screen organizes all of your photos into Years, Collections (which are logical groupings of photos that iOS puts together for you) and Memories (a thumbnail view of all of your photos). Move from Moments to Collections and from Collections to Years by tapping the text in the top left corner. Move from Years to Collections and Collections to Moments by tapping the photo sets.

From Moments, tap on any photo or video to view it, edit it, share it or delete it. For budding filmmakers, iOS 10 allows you to zoom in on your video footage.

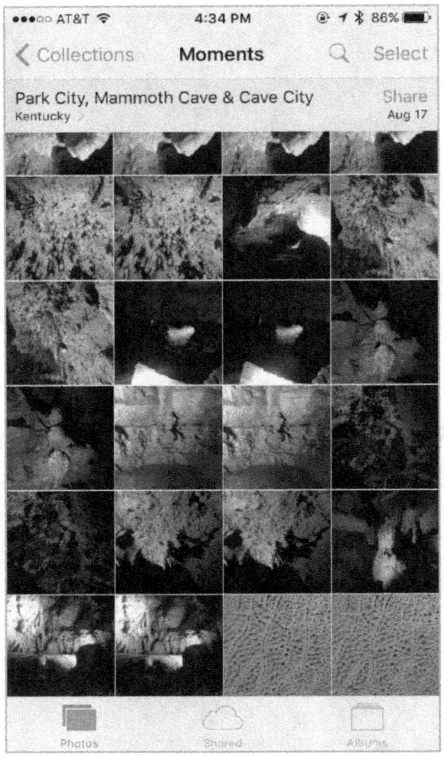

Screenshot 87: Moments in Photos

Memories is the newest feature released with iOS 10 for Photos, and it offers you lots of new and fun ways to share and view your photos and videos. Tapping on the Memories screen will highlight a Best of the Year, the most recent month, and the Best of the Last 3 Months, but the fun doesn't stop there. Tapping on any of these will bring up a new screen with a lot more options for you to enjoy. How does this all work? Photos scans your photo library to look for photos and videos grouped together to create memories. iPhone takes this technology even further by creating Memory movies, all set to music. Memories, of course, may vary depending on the types of photos and video you've taken but can include anything from special events, random scenes, to photos of family and friends.

When you tap into a specific Memory screen, you'll notice a video created specifically for that Memories screen. Set to music, it will feature all the highlights and photos shared in Photos. If you swipe down on your iPhone, you'll see individual photos, Groups & People, Places, Related, Add to Favorite Memories, and Deleted Memory.

This means you have lots of options to view your Memories in different ways. You can also create your own Memories video by creating a new album.

Screenshot 88: Memories by Date

Shared Photos include any albums you've shared with others or that others have shared with you. It's easy to set up a new shared album. Visit the Shared screen and then tap New Shared Album. Give the album a name and then select people to share it with. Next, select pictures to share. You can add pictures to this album at any time and they'll automatically appear in your selected contacts' Photos app. View all of the activity in your shared photos by tapping Activity at the top of the Shared screen.

Finally, the Albums screen displays any albums you've created, as well as some iOS 10 default albums, which are exactly what they sound like – All Photos, Bursts, People, Panoramas, Places, Recently Deleted, Selfies, Screenshots, Slo-Mo, and Videos. Some notable album additions in iOS 10 include People and Places. Photos scans the images and videos you take and groups together faces most frequently found in your People screen. This feature is found only on the 5S or higher and allows you to also tap albums and people to be added. You can also name people, merge people (if they are listed as separate individuals), and even remove misidentified people. The more you interact with it, the smarter the feature is!

In the Albums screen, you can view your photos grouped by location by tapping on Places. This will show a photomap view. Tap on a place to view all of the photos you took while you were there.

Screenshot 89: Photos Location Map

Photos will automatically add pictures taken with the front-facing camera to the Selfies album, making it easy to find your best selfie shots. Similarly, any screenshots you take (hint: hold down the Home button and the power button at the same time to take a screenshot) will be saved in the Screenshots album.

When you're looking at a photo, you'll also find a scrolling photo track underneath it (new to iOS 10), making it much easier to navigate a set of photos than the old method of switching back to the album view.

Screenshot 90: Viewing Photos

Using iCloud and iCloud Photo Library

With iCloud Photo Library, images that you take on another iOS device (such as your iPhone) are automatically synced to your computer and/or iPad, if Photo Stream is enabled. You can also view your photos on icloud.com from any computer with an internet connection. iCloud Photo Library is limited by your iCloud storage plan. The free plan that your iPhone ships with gives you 5MB of storage space, but expanded storage is surprisingly economical (see 4.15).

All photos stored in your iCloud Photo Library count against your iCloud storage limit, but My Photo Stream does not. My Photo Stream includes up to 1,000 of your latest photos for up to 30 days on other iOS devices. Your Mac computer can automatically import Photo Stream photos and store them permanently, meaning you can easily back up your iPhone photos without paying for additional cloud storage. To enable this, open the Photos app on your Mac and be sure that My Photo Stream and Automatic Import are enabled under Preferences.

Creating and Managing Photo Albums

To create a new album, tap the + in the top left corner of the Albums screen. Give your new album a name and then select the photos you want to include by tapping them. Tap Select and then Done to save the photos to the album.

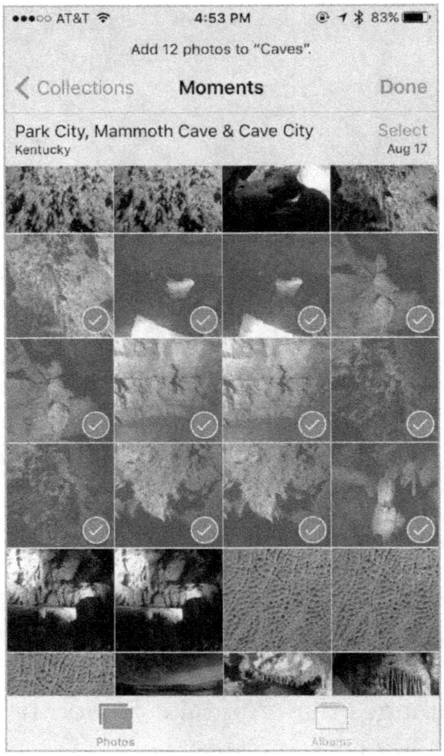

Screenshot 91: Selecting Photos for a New Album

To add photos to an existing album, tap Select in the top right corner of the screen. Select the photos you'd like to add by tapping them and then tap Add To at the bottom of the screen. Tap the appropriate album to finish the process. You can also create a new album by using Select and Add To – instead of choosing an existing album, scroll all the way to the bottom and tap New Album.

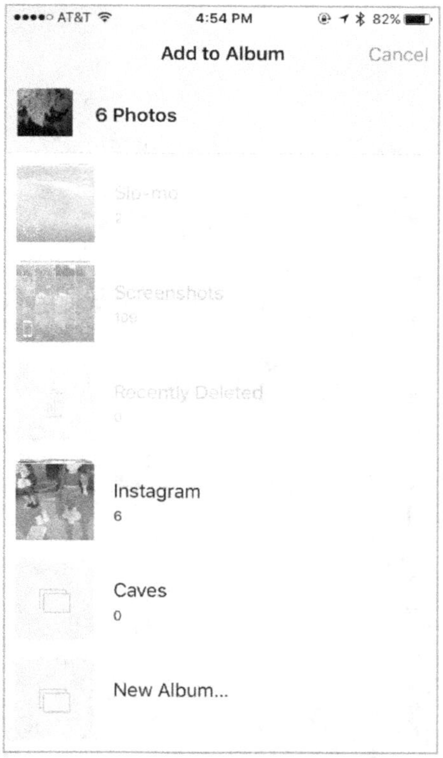

Screenshot 92: Adding Photos to an Existing Album or to a New Album

To manage your custom albums, tap Edit in the top right corner of the main Albums screen. To delete a custom album, tap the red circle that appears next to it. To move it, use the three lines that appear to the right of the album name to drag it up or down. To rename the album, tap its name to bring up the keyboard. You can only edit and delete custom albums.

Note: deleting an album does not delete the photos themselves.

Editing Photos

iOS 10 allows users to make a fairly broad selection of edits to an image directly in the Photos app. To access them, open a photo and tap Edit, located on the bottom of the photo screen. It now looks like three sets of lines with circles in them. At the bottom of the Edit screen, you'll see options to crop, add a filter, and adjust the brightness, color or saturation. In the top right corner, you'll see the magic wand icon for auto-enhancement, which will correct color balance, saturation and contrast for you automatically. After you've made your changes, tap Done if you're satisfied with your edits, and Cancel if you're not.

Screenshot 93: Edit Featured at the Bottom of the Photo Screen

Screenshot 94: Editing a Photo

New to Photos in iOS 10 is the ability to markup images. Add a bit of handwritten text or a smiley face. Let your creativity soar with these new features. Simply tap on the circle with three dots in the top left hand portion of your photo screen to select markup and other options. Tap on Markup. From there, you can write, draw, and zoom. When you are finished with your markup options, tap Done.

Screenshot 95: Adding Markup to a Photo

Sharing Photos

Photos can be shared individually by using the Share button in the bottom left when viewing a single photo. Photos can be shared through Messages, Mail, iCloud Photo Sharing, Twitter, Facebook, or Flickr, or you can assign photos to contacts, print them, copy them, or set them as your iPhone's wallpaper. Swipe right and left to see all of the sharing options available to you.

Screenshot 96: Photo Sharing Options

Searching and Favoriting Photos

iOS 10 includes a few other useful tools for finding photos. Use the heart in the bottom center of the screen to add a photo to the built-in Favorites album. Use the magnifying glass at the top of the Photos screen to search for places and dates. You can also use search suggestions as a fun, guided way to find the perfect Throwback Thursday post. In iOS 10, Siri can also help you search your photos. For example, you can say, "Show me photos from Florida last May," and Siri will pull up exactly what you're looking for.

Hiding Photos

In iOS 10, you can hide photos that you don't want to display. To do this, select the photo using the Select command in the top right corner of a photo display screen. Then tap the Share icon (counterintuitive, we know). Tap Hide and the photo will disappear. Hiding a photo will remove it from Moments, Collections and Years, but it will still appear in Albums.

Making a New Key Photo

Are you looking to make a new Key Photo? In iOS 10, it's easier than ever.

1. Open Photos

2. Tap the "Albums" tab, and find your image in Live Photos
3. Hit "Edit" in the top right corner of the selected image
4. Scrub through your Live Photo at the bottom of the screen and find the spot you want for a Key Photo
5. Hit "Make Key Photo"
6. Hit "Done"

And that's all there is to it.

iOS 10 Augmented Reality

Apps is able to use Apple's AR, or augmented reality, technology. ARKit is a new feature that allows you to experience immersive, adventurous experiences that blend realistic visual objects with the real world. This feature uses your phone's camera to deliver an onscreen, live view of the physical world. You see three-dimensional objects superimposed over the images of the physical world, creating a remarkable illusion. You can even reorient the device to explore things from different angles. It's possible to interact with these objects through gestures and movements.

3.9 Weather

Your iPhone includes a handy weather app so that the forecast is never more than a tap away. The iOS 10 interface features a beautiful graphical background to give you an idea of weather conditions at a glance. If it's raining outside, it'll be raining in your weather app as well.

The Weather app is fairly simple – it pulls data from The Weather Channel, and if you've enabled Location Services, it will show you the current conditions, hourly forecast and extended forecast for your current location. You can also see a full ten-day forecast, as well as sunrise and sunset information, by scrolling down.

Of course, you may want to know what the weather's like in other locations as well. You can set Weather up to give you information for multiple locations by tapping the menu icon in the lower right corner. This brings up a screen where you can add locations by tapping the + in the bottom left corner. This screen gives you the option to switch from Fahrenheit to Celsius using the two buttons near the bottom of the screen.

If you're keeping track of the weather in more than one location, swipe to the left or right to move through all of your saved Weather locations.

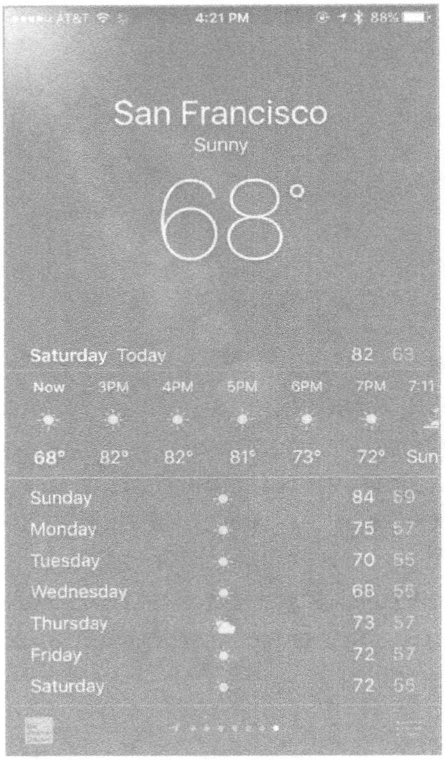

Screenshot 97: Weather App

3.10 Clock

The iPhone clock app is extremely handy – it includes a customizable world clock, an alarm, bedtime, a stopwatch and a timer, all of which work beautifully.

World Clock

The world clock allows you to create a list of locations and view the current time at a glance. This is particularly useful for anyone with friends, family or business partners in different time zones! To add places to the World Clock list, just tap the + in the top right corner.

Screenshot 98: World Clock

Alarm

Alarms can be set by tapping Alarm at the bottom of the screen, and then tapping the + button in the top right corner. This brings up the Add Alarm box. Adjust the time by swiping up and down the dials for hours and minutes (and don't forget about AM and PM!). You can also set the alarm to repeat every Monday, Tuesday, Wednesday, etc.

If you've had about enough of the default alarm tone, you can choose a different sound. You can also use Pick a Song to access your iTunes library or purchase ring tones from iTunes.

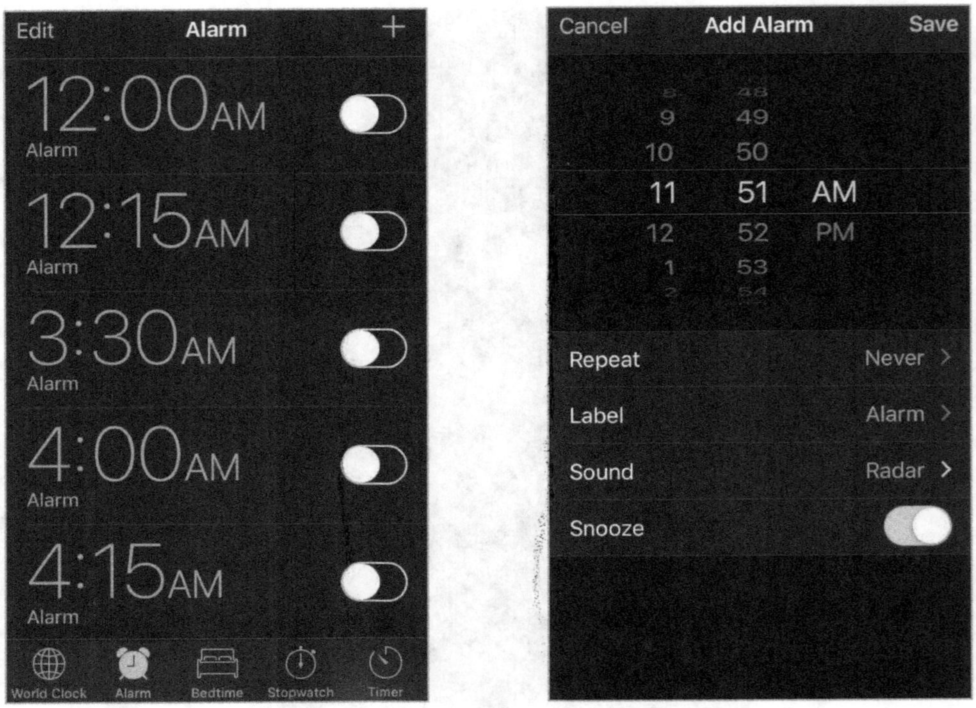

Screenshot 99: Setting a Repeating Alarm

To delete or adjust alarms, use the Edit button in the top left corner. This brings up a list of every saved alarm. Tap the red circle next to the alarm you want to delete to bring up the delete button, and then tap Delete. Or tap the Alarm time to adjust it as needed.

When your alarm sounds in the morning, unlock your phone to turn it off, or tap Tap to Snooze for a few more precious minutes.

Bedtime

Bedtime is a new feature to Clock in iOS 10. It lets you set the number of hours that you want to sleep each night, with reminders to go to bed and even wake up. This is a nice feature that goes beyond your typical alarm clock. You can easily customize when you want to go to sleep and wake up by tapping on Bedtime and adjusting the circular dial with your finger. You can set it for weekdays or adjust days as needed, depending on your schedule and preference. In addition to being a handy tool for keeping you on a well-rested sleep schedule, it also does a sleep analysis over the course of the week. Sleep analysis can be used not only in the Clock app but also in the Health app too (see 3.18)

Screenshot 100: Bedtime

Stopwatch

The iPhone Stopwatch consists of an elapsed time display, a Start/Stop button, and a Lap button. Tap Start to start the clock, and then use Lap to record a lap, and Stop to stop the clock. Laps are recorded underneath the elapsed time.

Screenshot 101: Stopwatch

Timer

The Timer feature lets you set the length of time you want to count down, and gives you buttons for starting and pausing the timer. Tap When Timer Ends to change the sound used when the timer is finished.

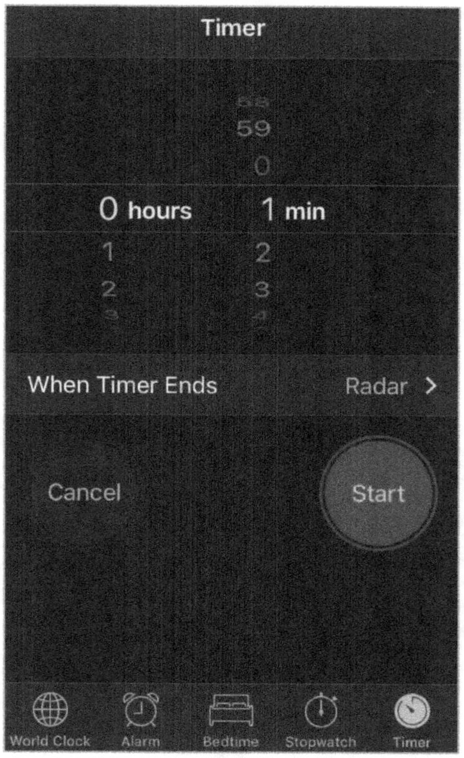

Screenshot 102: Timer

3.11 Maps

Maps is Apple's in-house answer to Google Maps (though of course, if you're a Google Maps devotee, you can always download the Google Maps app from the App Store). It makes use of Location Services to serve up relevant information based on your current location and includes a number of handy features like directions, satellite view, Yelp review integration, and more. iOS 10 also has the ability to navigate public transportation in several major cities, meaning it's never been easier to find your way around a new city. iOS 10 also offers a cleaner interface with larger buttons and easier to read font. To add to this, Maps can also now scan your calendar and recognize your routine and routes automatically. And, if you're prone to forgetting where your car is, Maps now has the ability to show your parked car location.

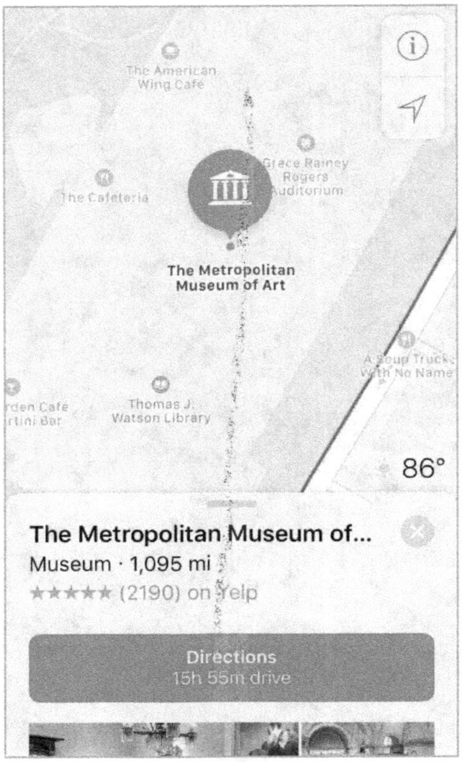

Screenshot 103: iPhone Maps

3D and Satellite View

If Location Services are enabled, Maps will reveal your current location with a blue dot when you tap the location arrow in the bottom left corner. You can also view the map area in 3D, if you're in a supported location, by tapping 3D. For more options, tap the circled i icon at the bottom. Here, you can change the view to a satellite or transit view, print, show or hide traffic, mark your location or add a place.

Tip: In iOS 10, 3D view is more difficult to find and is not readily visible in Maps. To view a 3D map, drag two fingers up. This works best in satellite view.

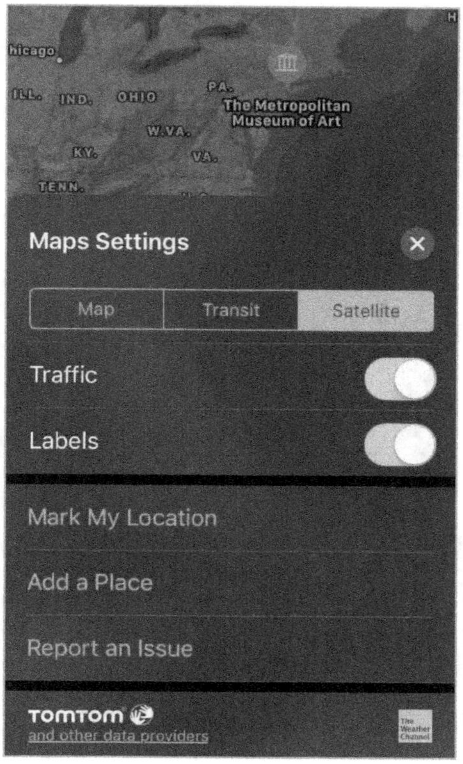

Screenshot 104: Maps Options

Places and Bookmarks

iPhone's Maps allow you to bookmark locations and learn more about them. Any time you see a location's name, swipe up to find out more about the place. You'll also have options to save the address in your Contacts, share the location, or add it to your Maps bookmarks (bookmarks in Maps are saved locations that you can access when you either search or get directions). Some locations will even allow you to purchase tickets using Apple Pay straight from the Maps app! Scroll down to see all the place options. Places also has better integration with Yelp and Wikipedia and includes reviews, Wikipedia entries, and photos.

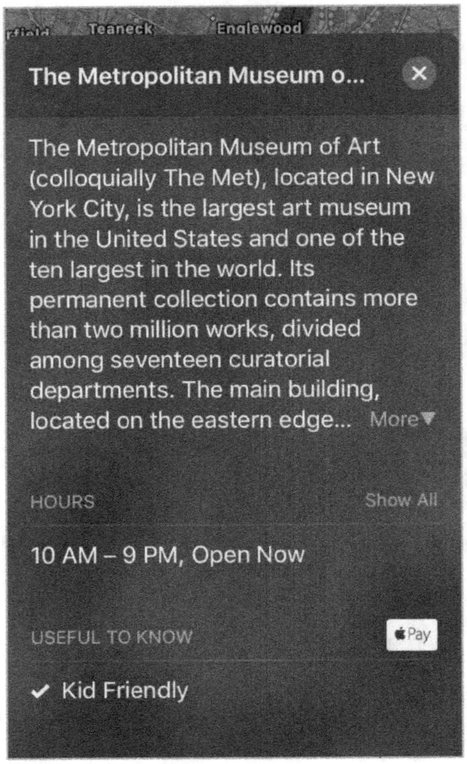

Screenshot 105: Place Information in Maps

Directions

To get turn-by-turn directions, touch the search box in the bottom of the screen. Search for your destination. Tap on Directions. Tap on My Location to change your current location. Notice that you can choose between walking, driving, public transit route, and ride options in iOS 10. If Transit view is available, it will also include schedules and other relevant information to help you accurately estimate how long your trip will take. Ride view connects you to Lyft and other popular ride options, such as Uber. In order to view Ride options, download ride apps in the App Store.

Tip: You can also get directions by asking Siri in iOS 10. You can use phrases like, "Hey Siri, can you tell me how to get to the Metropolitan Museum of Art?" or "Find a gas station."

Tap Go to start your trip! iOS 10 uses guided voice navigation so you never need to worry about missing your turn. You can always look over the full direction set by swiping up on your directions and then tapping on Overview in the bottom left corner. To end guided navigation, tap End in the bottom right corner.

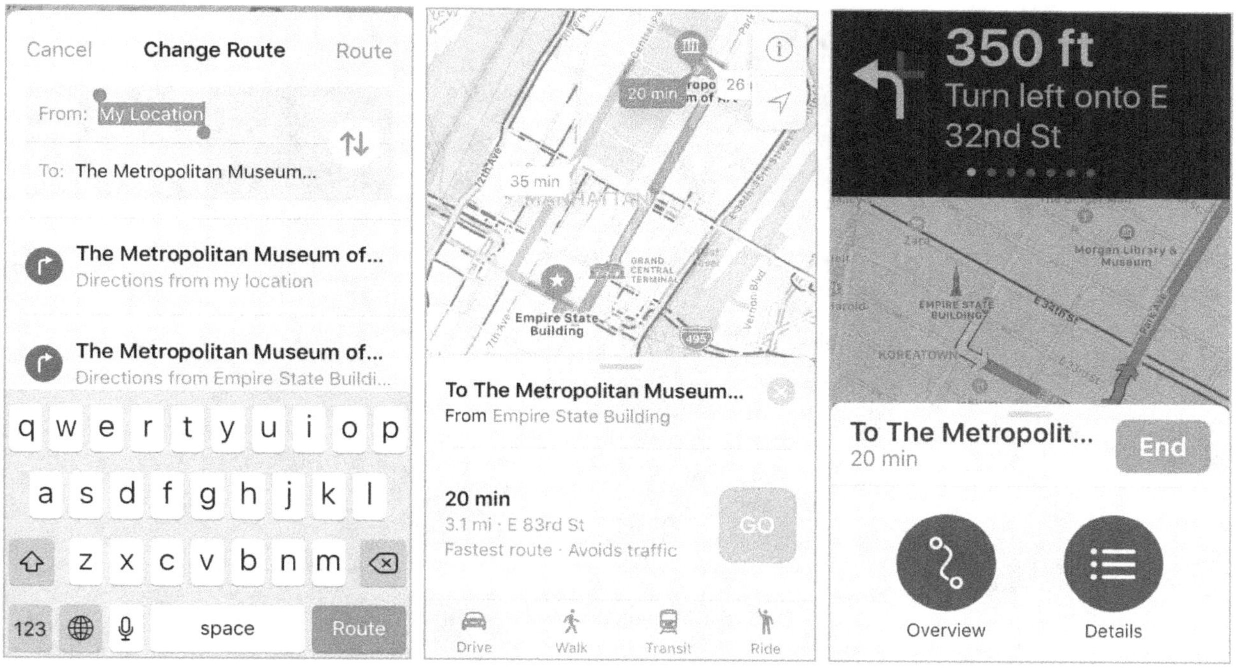

Screenshot 106: Directions in Maps

Nearby

Nearby is a new feature in iOS 10 Maps designed to help you explore an unfamiliar area. To use it, enter an address or use your current location. Then tap on the address bar. This will pull up the Nearby menu, which includes food, drinks, shopping, travel, services, fun, health and transport. You'll find subcategories in each main category. It's a great way to find the nearest coffee shop or shoe store.

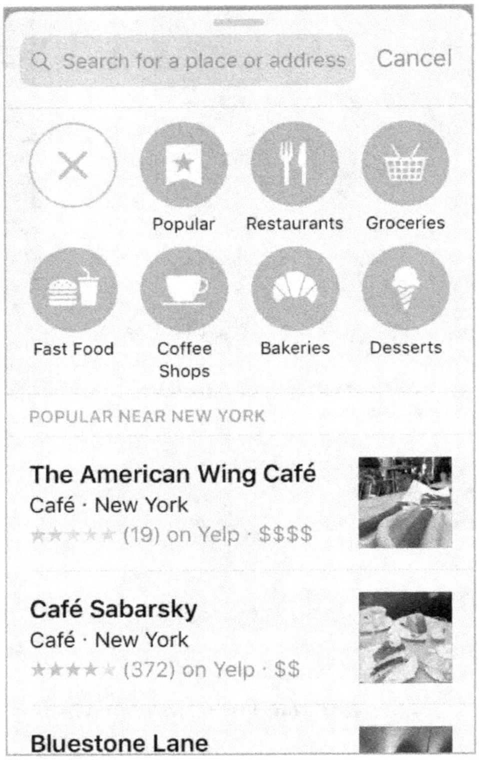

Screenshot 107: Nearby

Show Parked Location

For all those times you wish you had a better way to figure out where you parked, iOS 10 introduces a new feature that helps provide a solution to this age old dilemma. To enable this feature, you'll need to go to Settings > Maps > Show Parked Location. For it to work properly, you also need to a car with Bluetooth or CarPlay enabled. To find your car once Show Parked Location is enabled, tap the search field and look for Parked Car in the suggestions.

3.12 Notes

Notes has been an unobtrusive feature of iOS from the beginning. It's always been a handy scratch pad for jotting down quick thoughts and stray observations. However, in iOS 10, Notes has evolved from a handy utility into a full-featured productivity app that rivals the likes of Evernote and Wunderlist and has the ability for you to collaborate and share notes, making it an even more viable alternative to popular collaborative tools.

At first glance, there isn't much to Notes. At the bottom of Notes, you have some basic options, including a Share button, a Trash icon, and a New icon. Tap the New symbol to create a note, which will be synced across all of your iCloud-enabled devices.

Screenshot 108: Notes

In iOS 10, you'll find an additional menu in Notes just above the keyboard. Tap the + sign to reveal it. Here, you'll be able to add checklists, images and sketches, vastly extending Notes' usefulness.

Screenshot 109: Checklists and Sketches in Notes

You can also use Notes without typing by asking Siri. Tell her, "Note that I'm ready to start using Notes!" and watch what happens. Siri will add a new Note that you can read by opening the Notes app and tapping the Notes button in the top left corner. With iCloud, any notes you create will automatically sync across all enabled devices.

iOS 10 also adds Notes to the Share menu, meaning you can easily store pictures, maps, links and other content in Notes, helping you keep track of all of your ideas, inspiration, sources, etc. in one iCloud-enabled spot. Anything besides plain text is added as an attachment to a note. The Notes app also gives you an Attachments browser (the four small squares in the lower left corner of the main Notes screen), where you can see every attachment in your Notes app. This is useful when you start losing track of which note includes what information.

In iOS 10, you can also share Notes with friends, family, and co-workers. You can do this by tapping on the Share button at the top of the screen when viewing a note. From there, choose the way you want to send an invite for the note, add the contact person's name, and then send. It's that easy. Just like other collaborative tools, such as Evernote, anyone with access to the Note can make changes, add, or delete content. It's a great way to work together without having to add another app to your phone.

Do Not Disturb While Driving

iOS 10 introduces Do Not Disturb While Driving, a feature that mutes incoming calls, texts, and notifications while you're driving. This is perfect for cutting down on

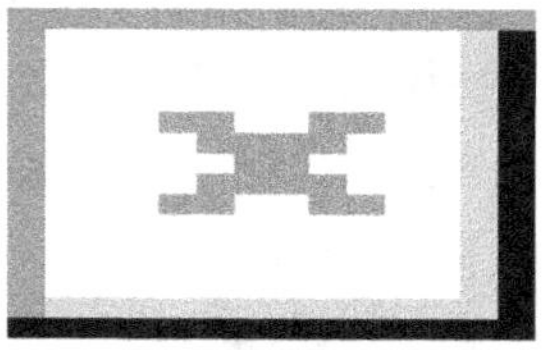

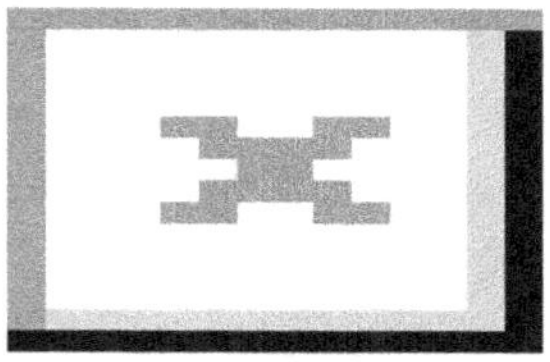

accident- causing distractions.

This feature is not embedded automatically, however. You will find a popup prompting you to turn it on when your phone detects the motion of a car. There are options for how you can use this feature if you miss the initial setup process. All in all, this can significantly add to your safety and the safety of others.

3.13 Reminders

If you're an obsessive to-do list kind of person, then Reminders is the app for you. It can import Tasks from Outlook or other similar programs, and you can create custom To-Do lists. Your iPhone will remind you through sounds, notifications, and badges that you've got things to do. Check off list items as you accomplish them.

Adding Reminders

To add a new reminder, just tap a line in the Reminders app and start typing. Enter a title for the reminder. If you want to add additional information, tap the little blue "i" next to the reminder. This will bring up a Details screen where you can ask your iPhone to remind you on a certain day at a certain time. You can also set a repeat reminder that will activate every day, week, two weeks, month and year by tapping Repeat. iPhone will also remind you to do things based on your location. Just turn on Remind Me At a Location, and enter the location. You can also prioritize your list so that the most important things get taken care of first.

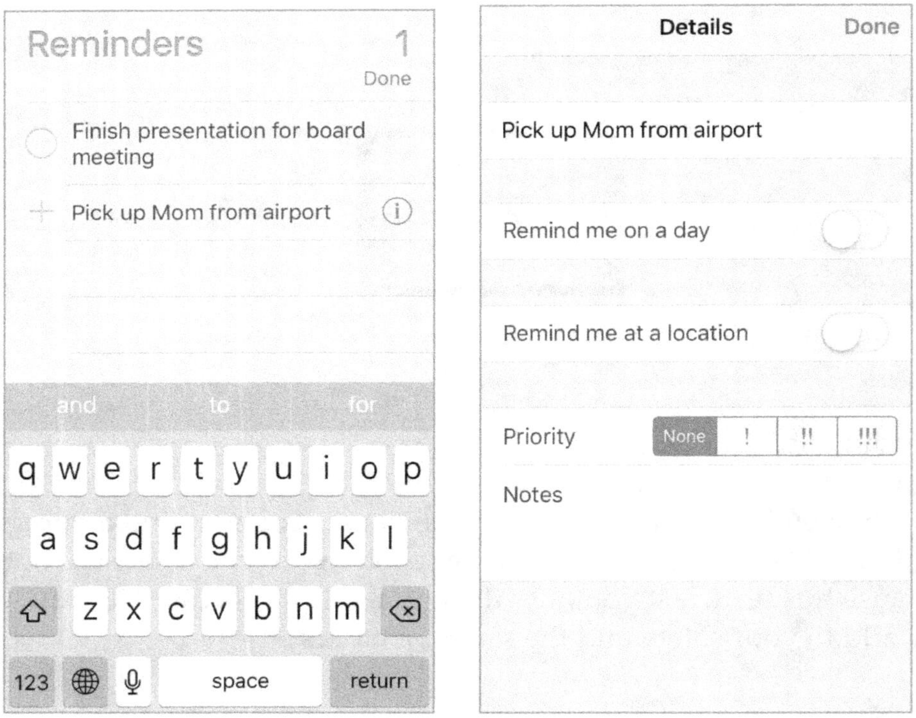

Screenshot 110: Setting Reminders

Managing Reminders

To delete reminders, tap Edit and then tap the red circle next to each reminder you want to delete. To mark a reminder complete (without deleting it), just tap the little circle next to it. You can also tap Completed in the left menu to view reminders you've already dealt with. You can organize your reminders into lists by tapping New List.

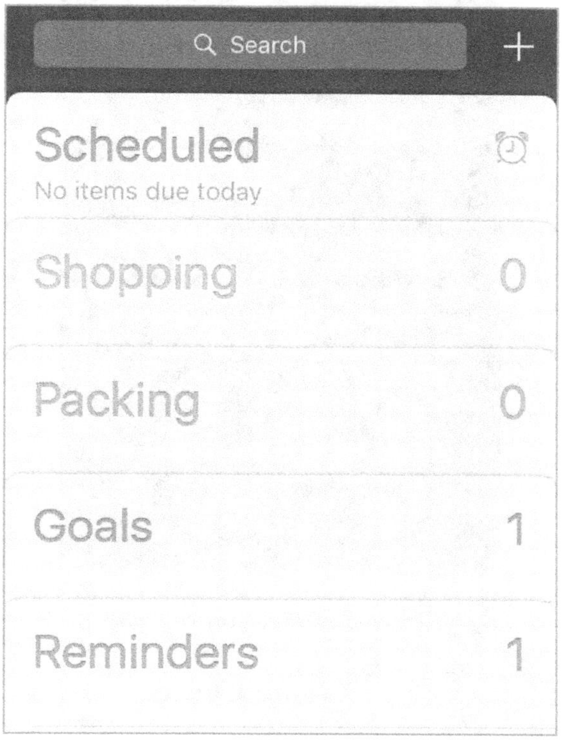

Screenshot 111: Adding a New Reminders List

iCloud will sync your reminders across all your iCloud-enabled devices. A word of warning: this can result in a lot of noise if you're in the same room with your iPad, iPhone, and Mac when a group of reminders starts buzzing!

If you've enabled Family Sharing, you can also make use of a special shared reminder list called Family. This list will be synced across all family members' devices. For more information on Family Sharing, check out Part 4.14.

3.14 Stocks

The iPhone includes Stocks, a customizable stocks tool. You can customize the stocks displayed by tapping the menu icon in the lower right corner. iCloud will sync your stocks data across all of your iCloud-enabled devices. Swipe the screen to the right and left to view the Dow Jones averages, rise and fall over time, and financial news headlines.

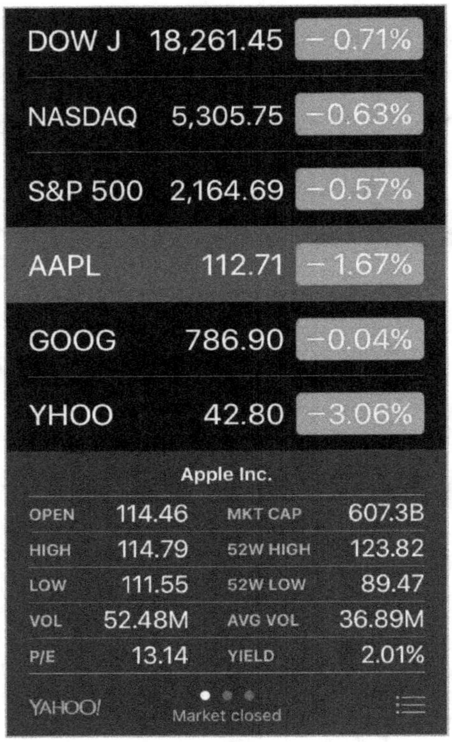

Screenshot 112: Stocks App

3.15 Game Center

Game Center is Apple's social gaming network. It lets you connect and play with friends (old and new) online, compete for top spots on leaderboards, and earn public points and achievements. If you have plans to play any social games on your iPhone, it's a good idea to set up a Game Center account. If you change or add iOS devices, you'll be able to keep your game contacts in the process.

Not every game available in the App Store is Game Center-enabled, though a large number are, including many of the most popular (Angry Birds, Plants versus Zombies, Clash of Clans, et al.). You can search Game Center games from within the Game Center app.

Once you sign in to Game Center, you'll be signed in permanently (unless you manually sign out). If you choose to opt out of Game Center and instead walk the path of the solitary Fruit Ninja, Game Center will pester you every time you open a Game Center game, reminding you that you're not signed in.

In iOS 10, there is no longer a Game Center app, so if you're used to using this in previous iOS versions, you've probably noticed it missing from your phone. But, don't despair gamers! You can still utilize all of the great Game Center features directly in individual games. Adding friends and inviting them to games will all be done in each specific game and then sent through Messages. You can also still find Game Center listed in your Settings.

3.16 News

News was brand new in iOS 9, and replaced the old Newsstand app. Rather than the app collection approach that Newsstand took to presenting periodicals on the iPhone, News embraces a magazine-style presentation that's similar to the popular Flipboard app. It's a perfect interface for consuming articles from your favorite news sources and magazines. In iOS 10, News is even better with a newly re-designed For You section, larger fonts, and bigger display. There's also increased subscription support for all your favorite major news publications.

When you first open News, you'll be asked to choose some sources to get you started. Choose from standards like CNN, Wired, Vox, etc. This will build a customized news feed for you that you'll find in the For You tab in the News app.

Screenshot 113: News for You

You can also explore topics and "channels" using the Explore tab, or search for information using Search. The topics list is enormous and includes just about any interest you might have. Adding favorites and reading stories will help News get to know your interests and preferences, and you'll find that your feed gets better and better the more that you use it.

Screenshot 114: Exploring in News

When you're reading a story in News, you'll find options to share, favorite, or save the story at the bottom of the screen. Favoriting stories that you enjoy will help News deliver the most relevant content to you. If you've found a long form article that looks interesting but you don't have time in the grocery store line to read the whole thing, just tap the bookmark icon. This will move the story to the Saved tab on the main screen so you can read it at your leisure. You also now have the option to dislike an article, which is another way to ensure that News delivers the most relevant content to you.

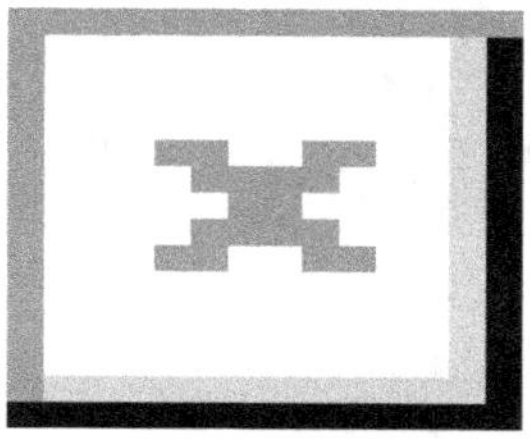

News App Improvements

The News app in iOS 10 has some remarkable improvements as well. The most notable one is "Today's View" where you can see all the most pertinent news stories of the day. That beats having to troll around Facebook looking for the most newsworthy videos.

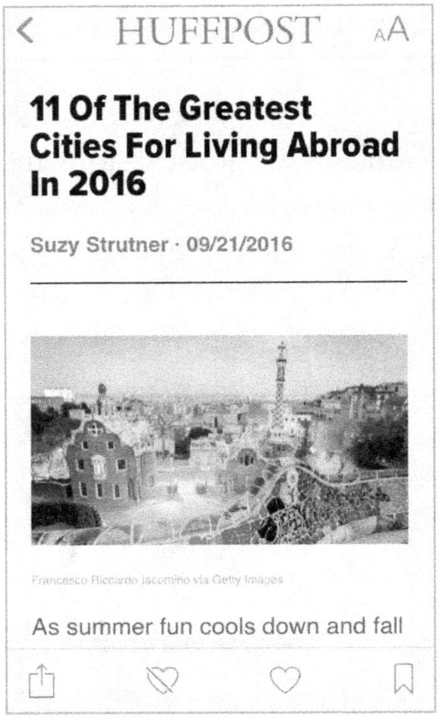

Screenshot 115: Reading View in News

3.17 iBooks

iBooks is Apple's answer to Amazon's Kindle platform. iBooks opens with the My Books bookshelves displayed. As in other Apple storefront apps, a toolbar at the bottom helps you navigate between your purchased books, featured items, top charts, Apple Store search, and Purchased Items. These functions work just like they do in iTunes and the App Store. Note that in iOS 10, Apple Audiobooks can be purchased and enjoyed through the iBooks app instead of iTunes / Music.

Screenshot 116: iBooks

Reading books in iBooks is similar to most other e-reading apps. Tap the right and left sides of the screen to turn pages, and tap in the center of the screen to display menu options. While inside a book, the menu icon will take you to the table of contents, the text icon allows you to resize the font for your reading comfort, the magnifying glass searches the whole book for words or phrases, and the bookmark icon allows you to bookmark specific pages for later. Your bookmarks are accessible using the menu icon at the top. At the bottom of the screen you'll see a progress bar and the number of pages left in each chapter.

Screenshot 117: Reading Alice in Wonderland by Lewis Carroll in iBooks

3.18 Health

The Health app was one of the most exciting new additions in iOS 8, and it has received some major upgrades in iOS 10 and is even more advanced than ever before. In iOS 9, we saw the introduction of a new reproductive health category, which approximately 50% of the human population needing to track certain monthly health events greatly appreciated! The update also included new metrics for keeping track of UV exposure and hydration. In iOS 10, Health now features 4 categories to keep track of: Activity, Mindfulness, Nutrition, and Sleep. Each has unique and new features, and all of them link to third party apps or Apple apps to increase the usefulness and accuracy.

Health makes use of Apple's new framework Health. Health is a means of collecting all of your health-related information – from steps taken to blood glucose measurement to nutrition data – in one customizable dashboard. Health is still fairly young, but many major fitness and health-related apps have integrated with it, including MyFitnessPal, RunKeeper, Clue and many others. Right now, Health functions more as a unified repository for health information that would otherwise be spread out across several sources, but it has a lot of possibilities in terms of health management, and we're definitely seeing some of the possibilities in iOS 10! Imagine being able to automatically sync blood pressure readings with your phone and then automatically send that information to your doctor. That's where Health is headed, and we're excited to see how much easier Apple will make our health data storage and sharing.

We'll be looking at some of the features of the Health app worth knowing about.

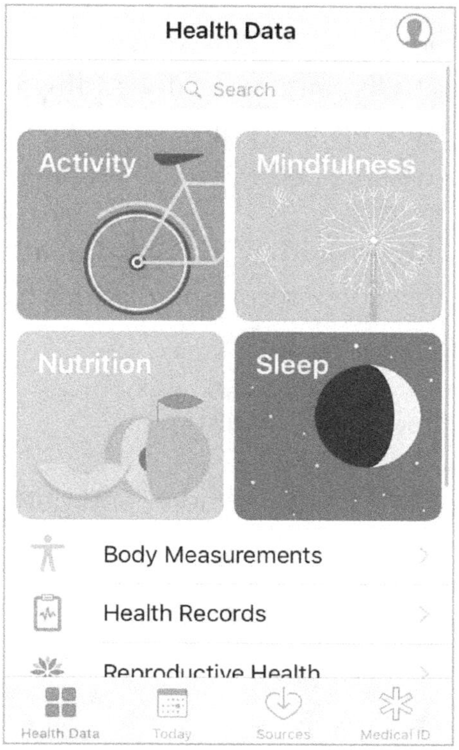

Screenshot 118: Health Dashboard

Navigating Health

The Health app includes a toolbar at the bottom with the following menu items: Health Data, Today, Sources, and Medical ID. The dashboard makes it easier than ever to get to the information you care the most about and is easy to find and view. Health Data lists the impressive variety of health information that Health can store for you. Whether you're focusing on your Activity or want to concentrate on Nutrition, the Dashboard makes each of these easily accessible and easy to use. You also have the ability to add medical records from your physician and add your daily vitals like blood pressure and heart rate. Each of the menu items allows you to view datasets by day, week, month, and year. You can also Show All Data to see a list view of your progress. Health now includes Data Sources & Access for third party apps and other Apple apps that might connect to Health.

Activity

Activity is the health data area that you might use the most. Keeping track of your workouts and steps are key components of Activity. Health includes a passive pedometer that measures your steps, distance travelled, and stairs climbed in the background, thanks to the M8 motion coprocessor chip in the iPhone 5s, iPhone 6 and iPhone Plus, the M9 chip in the 6S and 6S Plus, and the M10 chip in the 8 and 8 plus. This pedometer links up to Activity, automatically adding in your steps, as long as your iPhone is in your hand, armband, pocket, purse, or backpack. If you have your iPhone on hand and are moving, the passive pedometer is keeping track of steps and mileage.

Activity also gives you the ability to add in any physical activity manually or via a third party app. Activity will give you some recommendations for best apps to use in the Activity dashboard screen.

Screenshot 119: Health Activity Screen

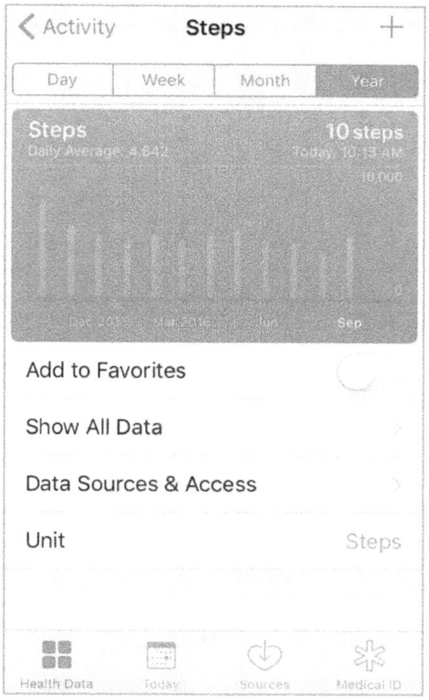

Screenshot 120: Health Data: Steps

If you're using a third party app, such as MyFitnessPal, you can choose to automatically add the built in pedometer to it too, adding even further integration of Activity and third party apps.

Nutrition

Nutrition works best with third party apps. Once you choose your preferred third party, make sure to adjust the settings so that data can be shared between the app and Health.

Screenshot 121: Health Nutrition Screen

Mindfulness

Mindfulness is another Health area that works best with third party apps. Of course, whether you're practicing yoga meditation or have a moment of mindfulness, you can easily add it yourself manually without the use of a third party app. So no matter where or when you're having a Zen moment, you can track it in whatever way works best for you.

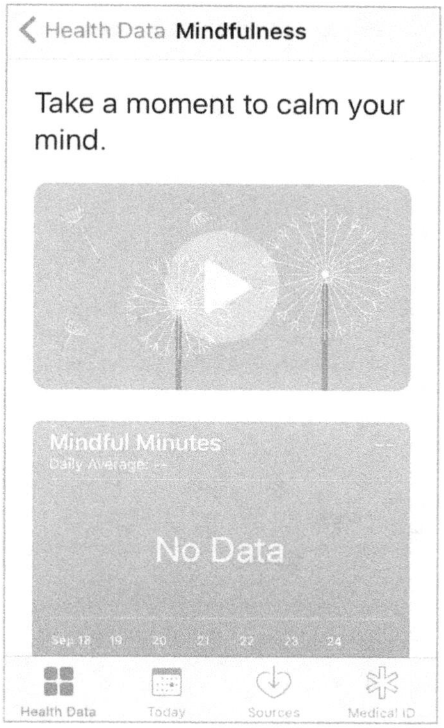

Screenshot 122: Health Mindfulness Screen

Sleep

One of the coolest new features in Health is Sleep. Though you can, of course, use third party apps, Sleep works just as easily and efficiently with Clock's new Bedtime feature. All you need to do is allow data to be shared from Bedtime in the Health app. This is can be done by tapping on Data Sources & Access and allowing access to Clock. This integration is another simple but highly useful way that iPhone is integrating new features of iOS 10 together.

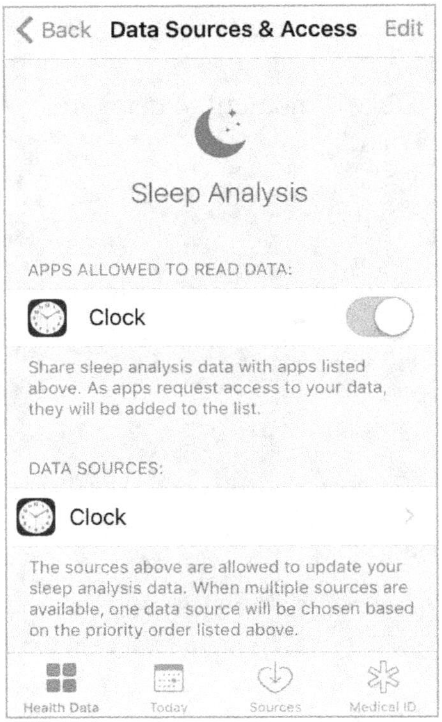

Screenshot 123: Health Sleep: Data Sources & Access

Today

On the main page of Health, you'll notice Today listed at the bottom of the screen. Tapping on this gives you information about your daily activity at a quick glance.

Screenshot 124: Health Today

Sources

Back on the main Health screen, Sources lists all of the apps and devices currently sharing information with Health.

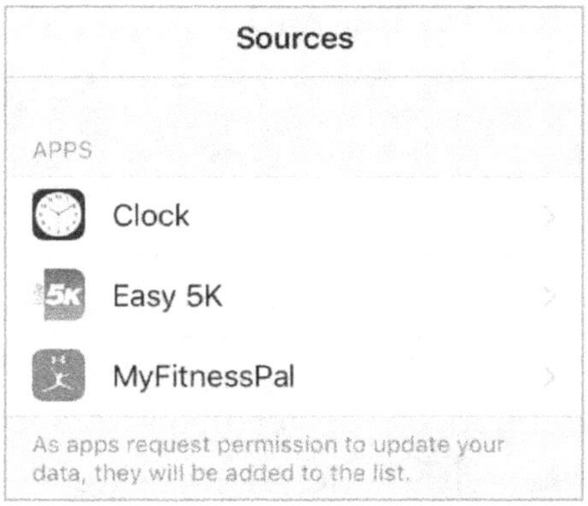

Screenshot 125: Health Sources

Medical ID

Finally, the Medical ID feature is useful, particularly if you have chronic conditions that you'd like to communicate to health providers, even if you're unable to speak yourself. Your medical ID might include medical conditions, allergies or medications that might impact care during an emergency situation. You can add as much or as little to your medical ID as you want. It will then be accessible by anyone from your lock screen. You can also now add Organ Donation directly in the Medical ID screen.

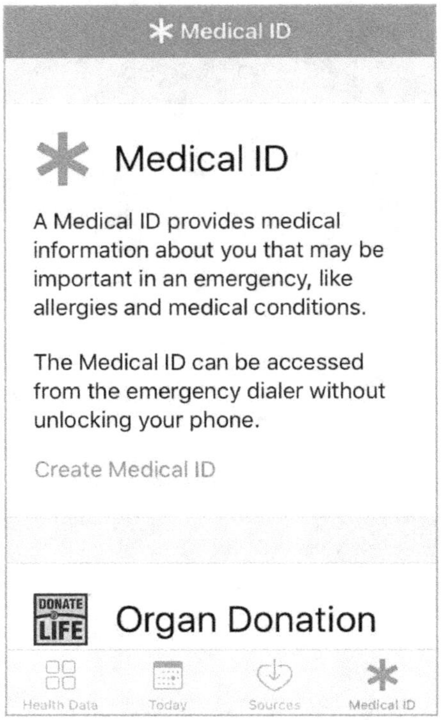

Screenshot 126: Health Medical ID

3.19 Wallet and Apple Pay

Wallet replaces Passbook, which was introduced in iOS 6. Wallet stores your Apple Pay credit card information (if you've chosen to enter it), as well as tickets, boarding passes, loyalty cards and/or coupons for easy access. There are quite a few apps that work closely with Wallet, including Sephora, Home Depot, most major airlines and many more. The Wallet app includes a link to Wallet-friendly apps in the App Store. Follow it to see if any of your regular retailers or service providers are listed! Note in iOS 10, Wallet and Apple Pay work best with Touch ID.

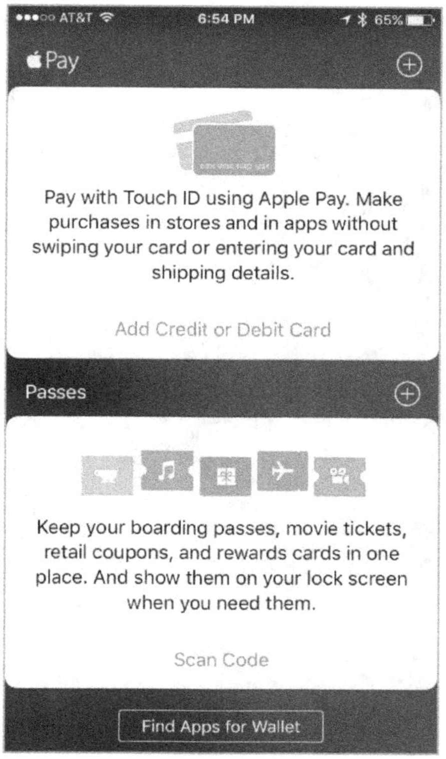

Screenshot 127: Wallet

When you've stored cards in your Wallet that are Apple Pay-compliant, you'll be able to use your iPhone to complete transactions in stores with contactless card readers. Simply holding your iPhone near the reader and using Touch ID to pay will allow you to make purchases without having to dig in your actual wallet for the card. Double clicking the Home button will open Wallet when your iPhone is locked. Apple Pay can also be used in-app for quick purchasing. Just select Apple Pay as a payment option.

You can set tickets or boarding passes to be visible on your lock screen by tapping the i icon. This is especially convenient in a busy airport!

3.20 FaceTime

FaceTime is Apple's famous video call service, and it's useful for families or friends who want to keep in touch with each other long distance. FaceTime doesn't count against your minutes, since it's an online service, like Skype. It works over 3G or Wi-Fi, meaning that if you have a limited data plan, you can still make unlimited FaceTime calls with a decent wireless connection.

Screenshot 128: FaceTime

The FaceTime app works similarly to the Phone app. You'll find your FaceTime favorites, your recent FaceTime calls, and your Contacts. To initiate a FaceTime call, tap on a contact's name. If you're camera-shy, you'll be glad to know that you have the option to switch to audio-only in FaceTime! Just tap on the telephone icon to initiate an audio-only call.

Screenshot 129: FaceTime Video and Audio Options

3.21 Calculator

Your iPhone comes equipped with a basic and scientific calculator. To reveal the scientific calculator, turn your iPhone to the landscape orientation. Calculator is also accessible from Control Center. Swipe up from the bottom of the screen and then tap the Calculator icon.

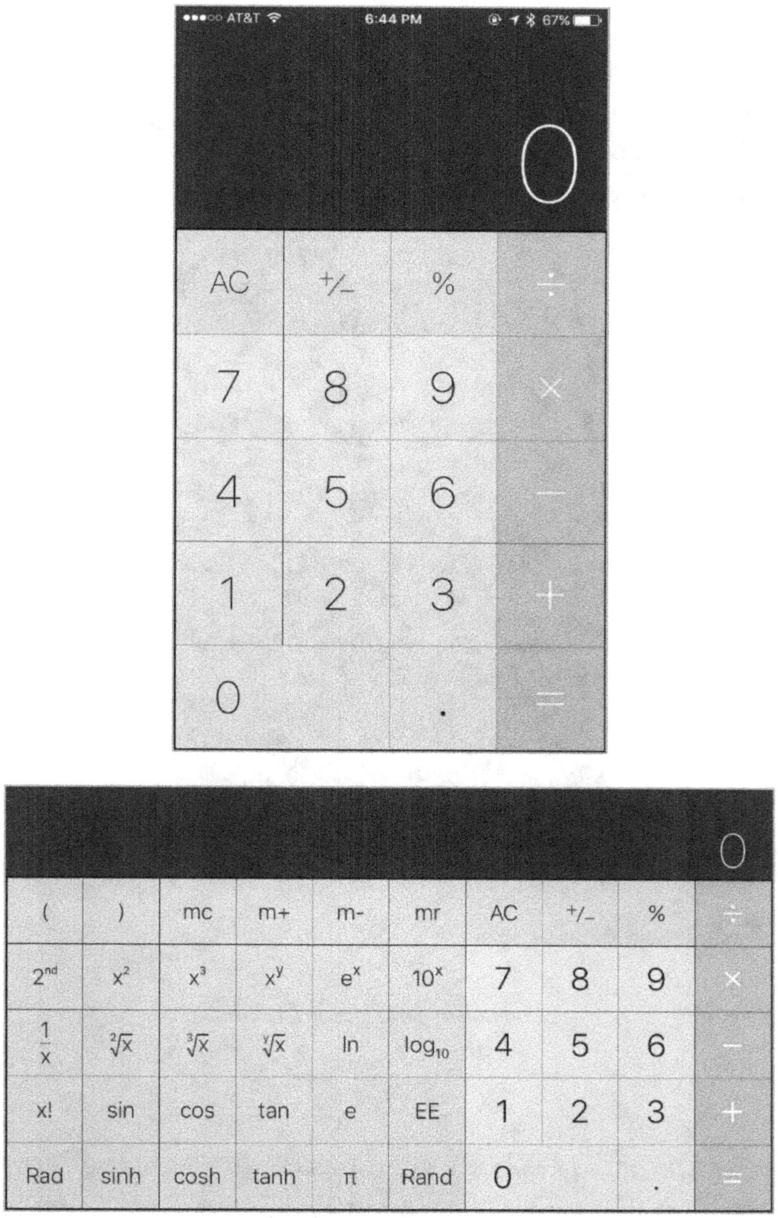

Screenshot 130: Calculator, in Portrait and Landscape Orientation

3.22 Extras

Your pre-loaded Extras app folder contains six small but useful apps – Compass, Tips, Voice Memos, Contacts, Find Friends and Find iPhone. If you find yourself using one of these apps frequently, you may want to move it out of the Extras folder and on to your home screen (see 2.3 to find out how to manage home screen folders).

Voice Memos

Think of Voice Memos as your iPhone's "note to self" machine. Press the record button in the bottom middle to record a memo. Then use the list icon in the bottom right corner to review, share and delete your memos.

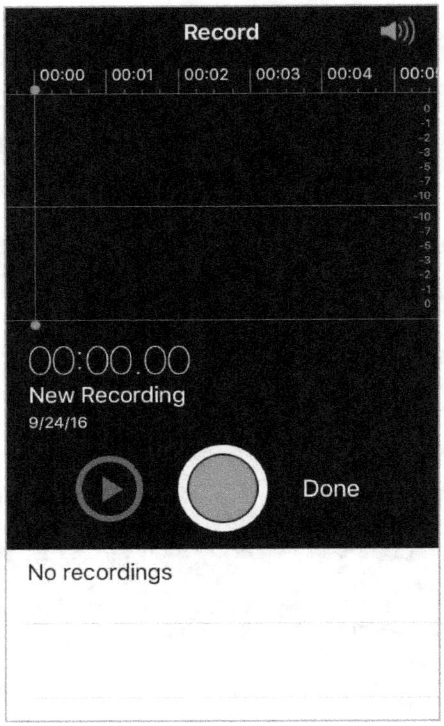

Screenshot 131: Voice Memos

Compass

The iPhone Compass app includes both a compass and a level tool, so you'll never need to worry about being lost in a forest of crooked picture frames. To calibrate the compass, follow the on-screen directions, and then head in whichever direction you need to go. Compass also displays your current latitude and longitude coordinates and your elevation. You can also swipe to the left to reveal iPhone's brand new level tool for all your picture-straightening needs.

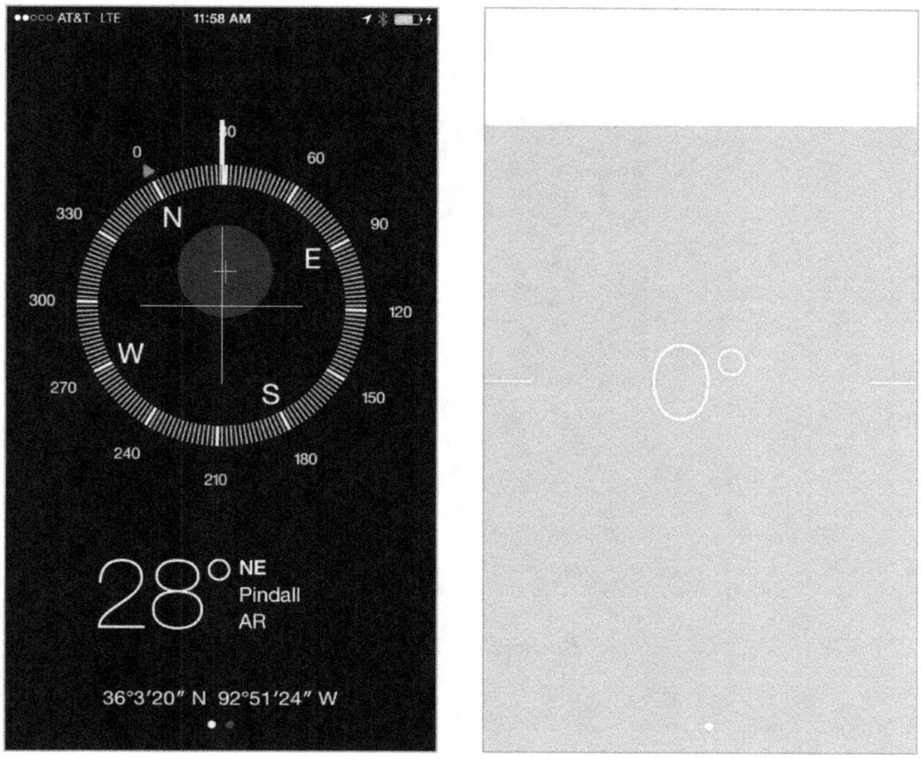

Screenshot 132: Compass and Level

Tips

Tips offers bite-sized bits of advice for using your new iPhone 8 and iOS 10. At the time of writing, there are five tip collection categories including: Featured, Everyday Essentials, Fantastic Photos, Mastering Messages, and Genius Picks, but expect Apple to update Tips regularly.

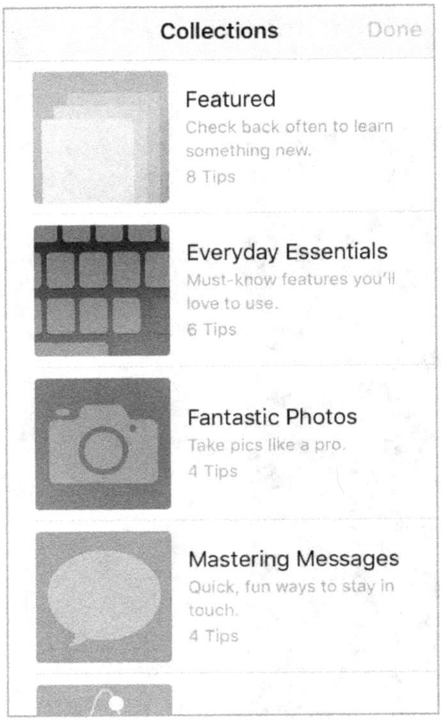

Screenshot 133: Tips

Contacts

We've covered Contacts in more detail when we talked about your Phone app way back in 3.1. However, you can also access your contacts here in your Extras folder. Whatever's easiest for you to use!

Find My Friends

Find My Friends is a social people finder app that can also be run as a widget in your Notifications center. The app displays a map that shows exactly where your friends are and how far away they are from you. You'll have to add friends using the Add function in the top right corner, and your friends will have to approve the service. You can even set up notifications that alert you when a friend leaves or arrives at a specified location by tapping a friend's icon in the app and then tapping Notify Me.

Screenshot 134: Notifications in Find My Friends

Find iPhone

Find iPhone is a useful app that allows you to see the location of all of your Apple devices on a map. You can remotely play sounds on devices (to help you find them under a pile of laundry, for example), send messages to them, and remotely erase them in case of theft. Of course, the app that's installed on your iPhone won't help you find your *iPhone*, but if your phone goes missing and you don't have any other Apple devices, just log on to icloud.com to see where your device has wandered to.

3.23 Watch and Activity

The Watch and Activity apps are tied to the Apple Watch. Unfortunately, without a paired Apple Watch, these two apps will just take up space on your home screen, and we recommend moving them to the Extras folder. If, however, you're fortunate enough to own an Apple Watch, the Watch app will help you pair and manage it and the Activity app will display all of the fitness stats your Watch collects for you.

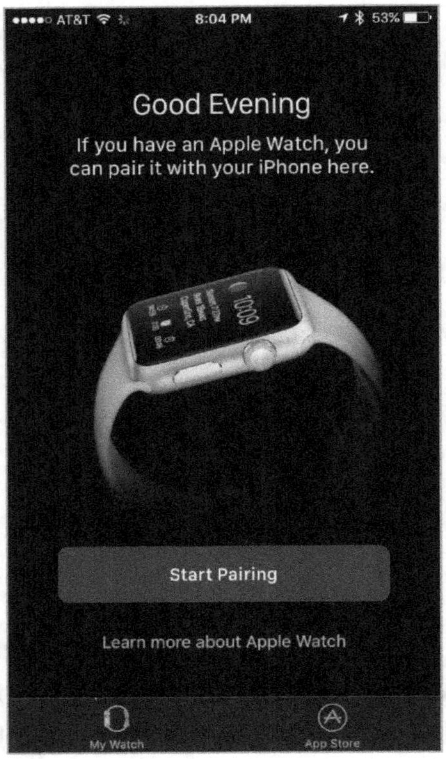

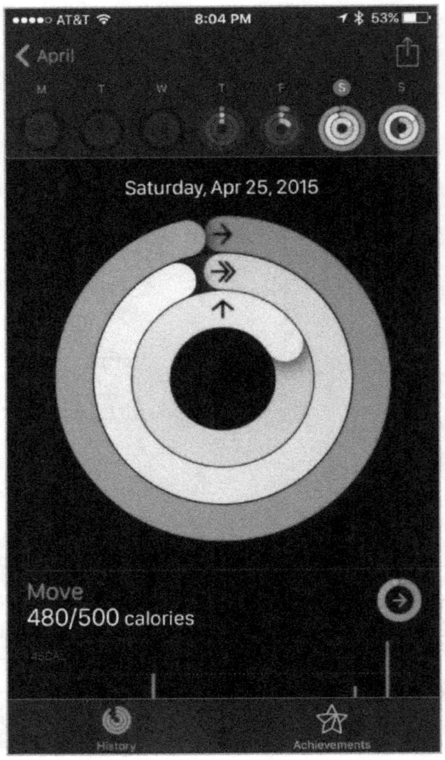

Screenshot 135: Watch and Activity

3.24 Home

We may have saved the best app for last with the newest app to launch in iOS 10 – Home. The Home app integrates HomeKit with iOS to help you better integrate all your home appliances and utilities, like lights, thermostats, refrigerators, and more. HomeKit uses Siri to control all of your smart home devices, which is a pretty handy tool, and the Home interface allows for a much cleaner and straight forward experience. To add your smart home device to Home, simply stand next to it with its power on and your Home app enabled. You can also use your 4th generation Apple TV to control HomeKit-enabled smart home devices.

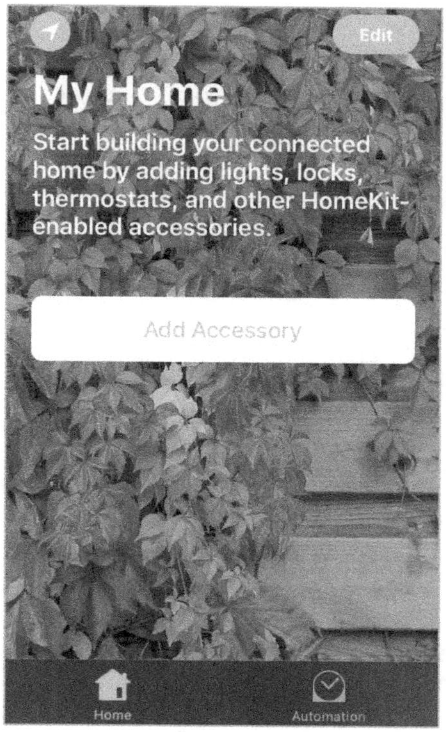

Screenshot 136: Home App

Wrap Up

Whew! That wraps up the pre-installed apps on your iPhone. If you think that's enough to keep you busy for a while, we certainly understand. You've probably also noticed that these apps are hardly self-contained - it seems like every app interacts with another app to provide the kind of unified, intuitive experience Apple is famous for.

As you move into the world of third party apps, you'll find that a large number of apps make use of your Contacts, Camera, Photos, Calendar, etc. In fact, in the next chapter, we'll set up Facebook, Twitter and Flickr, all of which can be deeply integrated into iOS 10 and all its functionality. If you're just starting out with your iPhone, it's a good idea to be sure you understand all of your pre-installed apps before you start downloading more – it'll give you a solid foundation not only for using other apps, but for understanding how they work.

Part 4: Making It Your Own

Getting your iPhone set up just the way you like it is one of the most fun aspects of new iPhone ownership. We've already discussed arranging your apps on your home screen and creating folders, and you've got an idea of how your apps work. Now let's take a look at other settings, personalization options and other advanced features available to you.

Most of this section will deal with your Settings area. You can access Settings from your home screen by tapping the Settings icon. You'll find Settings to be incredibly easy to navigate. You'll choose a category from the left menu and tap it to see available options. Everything is exactly where you'd expect it to be, for the most part. And if you can't find something, be sure to check Settings > General, where odds and ends tend to hide out, or use the new Settings search bar at the top of the Settings app – a great iOS 10 feature!

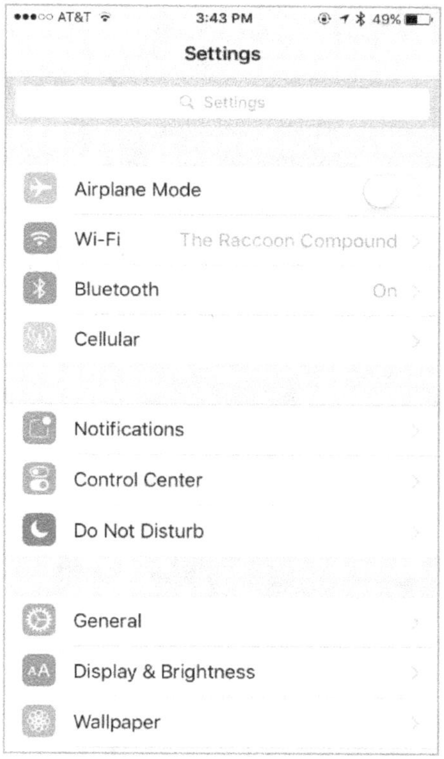

Screenshot 137: Settings

Tip: The Settings icon isn't the only graphic that uses gears. In plenty of apps, you can access additional app-specific settings by tapping gear icons in the app itself.

4.1 Do Not Disturb Mode

Do Not Disturb mode is a handy feature located near the top of your Settings app. When this operational mode is enabled, you won't receive any notifications and all of your calls will be silenced. This is a useful trick for those times when you can't afford to be distracted (and let's face it, your iPhone is as communicative as they come, and sometimes you'll need to have some peace and quiet!). Clock alarms will still sound.

To turn on, schedule and customize Do Not Disturb, just tap on Do Not Disturb in Settings. You can schedule automatic times to activate this feature, like your work hours, for example. You can also specify certain callers who should be allowed when your phone is set to Do Not Disturb. This way, your mother can still get through, but you won't have to hear every incoming email. To do this, use the Allow Call From command in Do Not Disturb settings.

Do Not Disturb is also accessible through the Control Center (swipe up from the bottom of the screen to access it at any time).

4.2 Notifications and Widgets

Notifications are one of the most useful features on the iPhone, but chances are you won't need to be informed of every single event that's set as a default in your Notifications Center. To adjust Notifications preferences, go to Settings > Notifications.

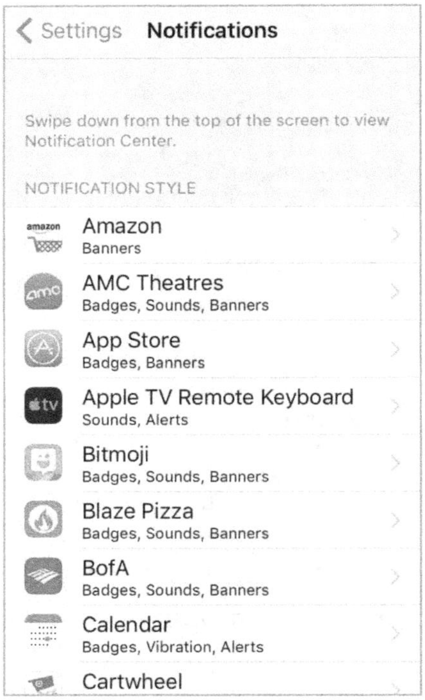

Screenshot 138: Notifications Settings

iOS 10 defaults to grouping your notifications alphabetically. You'll also see a list of all of the apps currently in your Notifications Center. By tapping the app, you can turn Notifications off or on and finesse the type of notification from each app. It's a good idea to whittle this list down to the apps that you truly want to be notified from - for example, if you're not an investor, turn off Stocks! Reducing the number of sounds your iPhone makes can also reduce phone-related frazzledness. For example, in Mail, you may want your phone to make a sound when you receive email from someone on your VIP list but to only display badges for other, less important email.

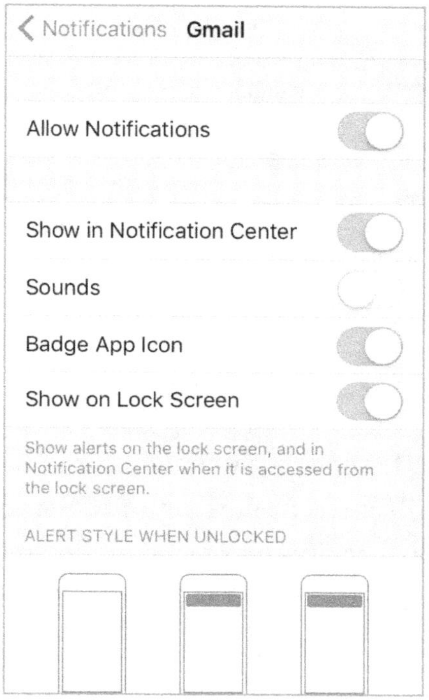

Screenshot 139: Customizing Notification Settings in Mail

You can also customize the widgets that appear in the Notifications Today panel. To do this, open Notifications by swiping up from the top of the screen. At the bottom of the Notifications Today tab, tap Edit. From there, you can remove widgets or add new ones. Note that widgets are now open to third party developers, so some of your favorite apps may include widget versions. They will automatically appear under More Widgets heading in the Today Edit screen. To enable them, tap the green plus sign.

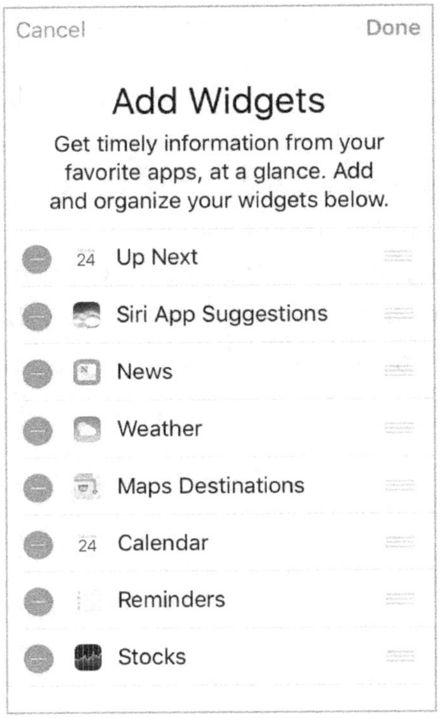

Screenshot 140: Editing Notifications Widgets

4.3 General Settings

The General menu item is a little bit of a catchall. This is where you'll find information about your iPhone, including its current version of iOS and any available software updates. Fortunately, iOS 10 ushers in an era of smaller, more efficient updates, so you won't find yourself scrambling to delete apps in order to make space for the latest improvements. You can also check your phone and iCloud storage here.

This is also where you can adjust some of the decisions you made when you set up your iPhone way back in 1.6. You can turn Siri on or off, or change its gender, set the date and time and set international options (like language and region).

The Accessibility options are located here as well. You can set your iPhone according to your needs with Zoom, Voiceover, large text, color adjustment, and more. There are a quite a few Accessibility options that can make iOS 10 easy for everyone to use, including Grayscale View and improved Zoom options.

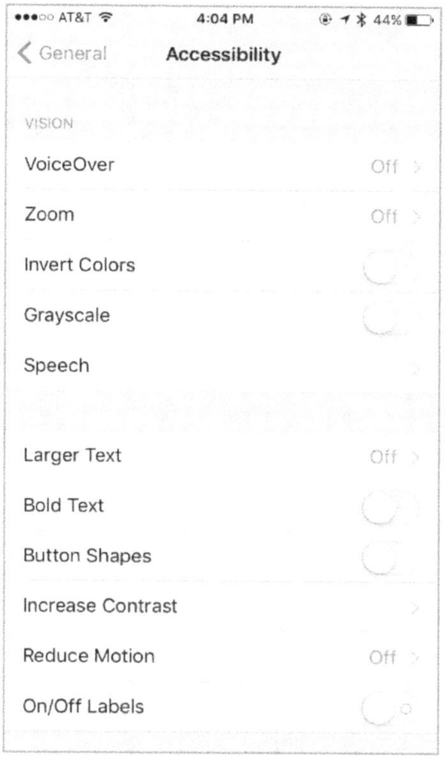

Screenshot 141: Accessibility Options in General Settings

A handy Accessibility option that's a little disguised is the Assistive Touch setting. This gives you a menu that helps you access device-level functions. Enabling it brings up a floating menu designed to help users who have difficulty with screen gestures like swiping or with manipulating the iPhone's physical buttons. Another feature for those with visual needs is Magnifier. Turning this on allows your camera to magnify things, and you can also click the home button and magnify anything that you're looking at.

We recommend taking some time and tapping through the General area, just so you know where everything is!

4.4 Battery

The Battery heading in your Settings gives you useful information about your device's battery usage. This is where you can enable Low Power mode to preserve battery life. You can also see which apps are using the highest percentage of your battery. Tap the clock icon to see how much time you've spent in each app to help you understand exactly how battery-hungry any given app is (and how much of your life each app is controlling!). For more tips on preserving battery life, skip ahead to 5.1.

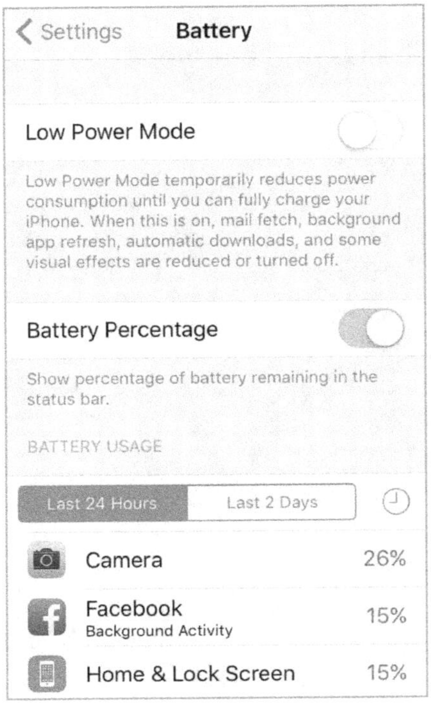

Screenshot 142: Battery Usage Monitoring

4.5 Cellular

The Cellular Settings area shows you whether or not data is enabled. This is also where you can check your usage and set up a personal hotspot (note that this will be carrier-dependent). You can also decide which apps you'd like to use cellular data and which ones should require Wi-Fi. This is a powerful way to make sure you stay within your data plan limits.

iOS 10 also includes a great feature here called Wi-Fi Assist. This will allow your iPhone to rely on cellular data when the Wi-Fi signal isn't great – perfect for those frustrating one-bar situations. Scroll all the way to the bottom of the cellular screen to enable or disable it.

4.6 Sounds

Hate that vibration when your phone rings? Want to change your ring tone? Head to the Sounds Settings menu! Here you can turn vibration on or off and assign ring tones to a number of iPhone functions. We do suggest finding an isolated space before you start trying out all the different sound settings – it's fun, but possibly a major annoyance to those unlucky enough not to be playing with their own new iPhone!

Tip: You can apply individual ringtones and message alerts to your contacts. Just go to the person's contact screen in Contacts, tap Edit, and tap Assign Ringtone.

4.7 Customizing Brightness and Wallpaper

On the iPhone, wallpaper refers to the background image on your home screen and to the image displayed when your iPhone is locked (lock screen). You can change either image using two methods.

For the first method, visit Settings > Wallpapers. You'll see a preview of your current wallpaper and lock screen here. Tap Choose a New Wallpaper. From there, you can choose a pre-loaded dynamic (moving) or still image, or choose one of your own photos. Once you've chosen an image, you'll see a preview of the image as a lock screen. Here, you can turn off Perspective Zoom, which makes the image appear to shift as you tilt your phone) if you like. Tap Set to continue. Then choose whether to set the image as the lock screen, home screen, or both.

Screenshot 143: Changing the Wallpaper Through Settings

The other way to make the change is through your Photo app. Find the photo you'd like to set as a wallpaper image and tap the Share button. You'll be given a choice to set an image as a background, a lock screen, or both.

If you want to use images from the web, it's fairly easy. Just press and hold the image until the Save Image / Copy / Cancel message comes up. Saving the image will save it to your Recently Added photos in the Photos app.

True Tone Technology

True Tone is a phenomenal upgrade to iOS 10 which adjusts the white balance onscreen to match the color temperature of light that is naturally around you. This works whether you're in overhead lighting or in direct sunlight. This technology fools your eye into thinking the screen looks white like paper, even as natural lighting changes.

What True Tone does is that it gives you a more natural looking display, which in turn, reduces eyestrain. Reading text is more comfortable than ever in all kinds of environments, and only the iPhone 8 and iPhone 8 Plus have it.

True Tone operates using sensors in your phone that constantly measure the intensity and tone of ambient light. iOS 10 uses this information to shift the white point of the screen, naturally and subtly. You can control True Tone in the Control Center of your iPhone 8.

1. Swipe up from the bottom edge of your iPhone 8 and pull up the Control Center.
2. Using 3D Touch, press the brightness bar.

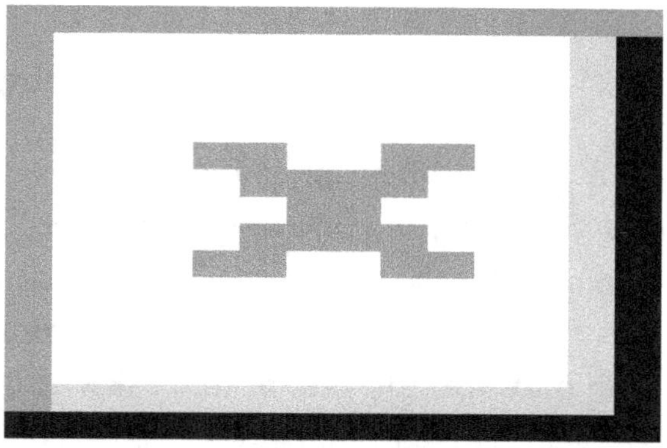

3. Tap True Tone below the slider, and toggle the feature on and off.

Side Note: It's also possible to toggle Night Shift from here. Enable or disable True Tone in Settings > Display & Brightness.

4.8 Privacy

The Privacy heading in Settings lets you know what apps are doing with your data. Every app you've allowed to use Location Services will show up under Location Services (and you can toggle Location Services off and on for individual apps or for your whole device here as well). You can also go through your apps to check what information each one is receiving and transmitting.

4.9 iCloud Settings

You can adjust what features are iCloud-enabled and what features aren't in the iCloud settings page. This may be useful if you have your own iPhone, but share an iPad with other family members and don't want to enable your iCloud mail on the shared device. You can also manage your iCloud backup settings here and keep track of friends and family with whom you've shared your location. You'll also find a heading for iCloud Drive here where you can enable the iCloud Drive app if you like. For more on iCloud Drive, see 4.15.

4.10 Mail, Contacts, Calendars Settings

If you need to add additional mail, contacts or calendar accounts, tap Settings > Mail, Contacts and Calendars to do so. It's more or less the same process as adding a new account in-app. You can also adjust other settings here, including your email signature for each linked account. This is also a good place to check which aspects of each account are linked – for example, you may want to link your Tasks, Calendars and Mail from Exchange, but not your Contacts. You can manage all of this here.

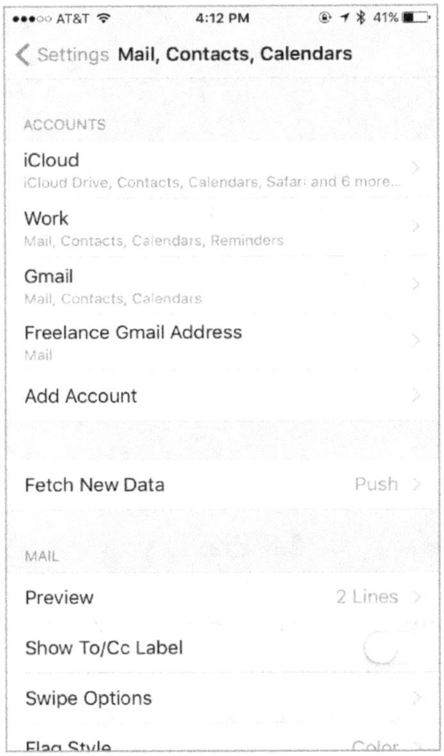

Screenshot 144: Managing Accounts in Settings

There are a number of other useful settings here, including the frequency you want your accounts to check for mail (Push, the default, being the hardest on your battery life). You can also turn on features like Ask Before Deleting and adjust the day of the week you'd like your calendar to start on.

4.11 Miscellaneous App Settings

Many apps will show up in your Settings menu with various options. For example, this is where you can clear Safari's browser history, disable FaceTime, turn off voice guidance in Maps, etc. We recommend taking some time to go through each app to see what you can do here. You can also sign in and out of the iTunes and App Stores here.

4.12 Adding Facebook, Twitter and Flickr Accounts

If you use Twitter, Facebook or Flickr, you'll probably want to integrate them with your iPhone. This is a snap to do. Just tap on Settings and look for Twitter, Facebook and Flickr in the main menu (you can also integrate Vimeo and Weibo accounts if you have them). Tap on the platform you want to integrate. From there, you'll enter your user name and password. Doing this will allow you to share webpages, photos, notes, App Store pages, music and more straight from your iPhone's native apps.

iPhone will ask you if you'd like to download the free Facebook, Twitter and Flickr apps when you configure your accounts if you haven't already done so. We recommend doing this – the apps are easy to use, free, and look great.

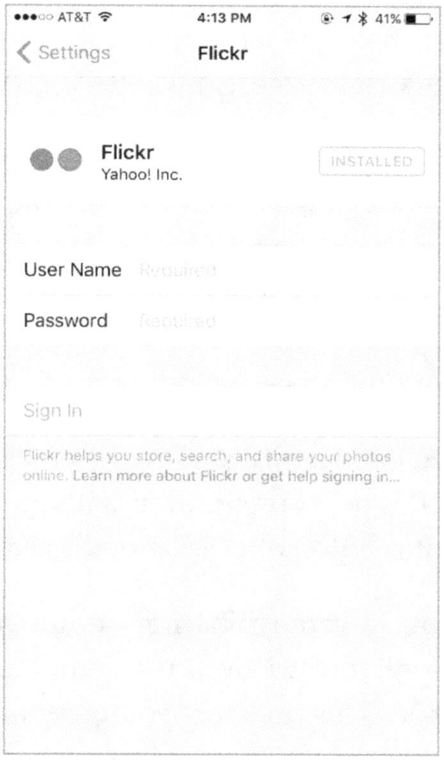

Screenshot 145: Integrating a Flickr Account

We found that when we associated our Facebook accounts, our contact list got extremely bloated. If you don't want to include your Facebook friends in your contacts list, adjust the list of applications that can access your Contacts in Settings > Facebook.

4.13 Resetting Your iPhone

If you're looking for the big red emergency button, this is it. In Settings > General > Reset, you'll find the options to reset all of the phone's settings or to erase all content and settings (restore to factory settings). Less drastic options include a network reset, resetting the dictionary, resetting the home screen, and resetting location and privacy settings. These options are useful when something goes wrong, but remember that any data lost during a reset cannot be recovered, so proceed with caution!

4.14 Family Sharing

Family Sharing is one of our favorite iOS 10 features. Family Sharing allows you to share App Store and iTunes purchases with family members (previously, accomplishing this required a tricky and not-entirely-in-compliance-with-terms-of-service dance). Turning on Family Sharing also creates a shared family calendar, photo album, and reminder list. Family members can also see each other's location in Apple's free Find My Friends app and check the location of each other's devices in the free Find iPhone app. Overall, Family Sharing is a great way to keep everyone entertained and in sync! You can include up to six people in Family Sharing.

To enable Family Sharing, go to Settings > iCloud. Here, tap Set Up Family Sharing to get started. The person who initiates Family Sharing for a family is known as the family organizer. It's an important role, since every purchase made by family members will be made using the family organizer's credit card! Once you set up your family, they'll also be able to download your past purchases, including music, movies, books, and apps.

Invite your family members to join Family Sharing by entering their Apple IDs. As a parent, you can create Apple IDs for your children with parental consent. When you create a new child Apple ID, it is automatically added to Family Sharing.

There are two types of accounts in Family Sharing – adult and child. As you'd expect, child accounts have more potential restrictions than adult accounts do. Of special interest is the Ask to Buy option. This prevents younger family members from running up the family organizer's credit card bill by requiring parental authorization for purchases. The family organizer can also designate other adults in the family as capable of authorizing purchases on children's devices.

If you'd like to further lock down your children's iOS devices, be sure to take a look at 5.2 for information about setting up additional restrictions!

4.15 iCloud Drive

iCloud Drive is a cloud storage solution similar to Dropbox, and it's better than ever in iOS 10. iCloud Drive offers wireless file sharing and syncing between compatible devices. iCloud Drive support is built into OSX Sierra and Yosemite, but it won't work with earlier versions of Mac OSX. iCloud Drive will share files from your apps, including the iWork Suite, as well as any other file type used on your computer. You can monitor which apps are sharing files with iCloud Drive in Settings > iCloud > iCloud Drive.

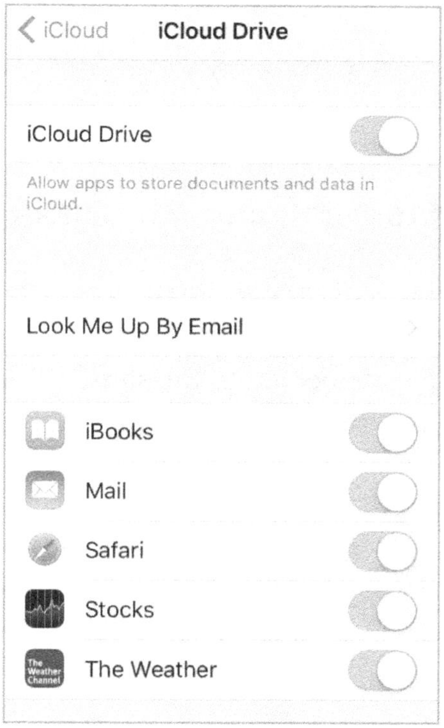

Screenshot 146: iCloud Drive Settings

iOS 10 includes a full iCloud Drive app (head to the iCloud Drive settings to enable it). This is a huge leap forward for iOS, which has never had anything resembling a file browser before. In the iCloud Drive app, you'll find all of your stored files in one place. Tap on them to open them in the appropriate app.

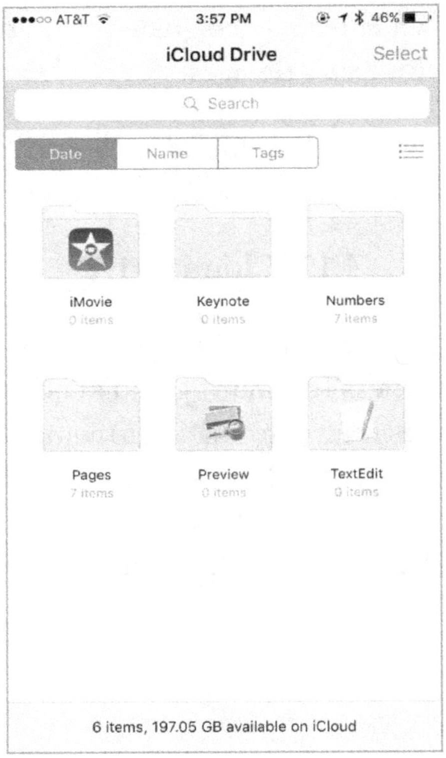

Screenshot 147: iCloud Drive App

4.16 Continuity and Handoff

iOS 10 includes some incredible features for those of us who work on multiple iOS 10 and Sierra and Yosemite OSX devices. Now, when your computer is running Yosemite or higher or your iOS 10 iPad is connected to the same Wi-Fi network as your iOS 10 iPhone, you can answer calls or send text messages (both iMessages and regular SMS messages) from your iPad or computer.

The Handoff feature is present in apps like Numbers, Safari, Mail and many more. Handoff allows you to leave an app in one device mid-action and pick up right where you left off on a different device. It makes life much easier for those of us living a multi-gadget lifestyle.

4.17 HomeKit and CarPlay

HomeKit and CarPlay are baked into your iPhone 8 so that it's ready to help you manage your home and integrate smoothly with your car's computerized system. HomeKit will work with anything that has a "Works with Apple HomeKit" sticker on the box. This includes lights, thermostats, garage door openers, locks, and much, much more. HomeKit devices can bring you all kinds of control and peace of mind.

Similarly, CarPlay technology ensures that your iPhone plays nicely with your car's system by replicating key apps on your car's display. For example, you can use CarPlay to get directions, listen to music through your iPhone, make calls, or send text messages, all without needing to pick up and navigate your iPhone (a decisively unsafe practice while driving). You can use CarPlay's features with your car's hardware - displays, steering wheel controls, knobs, etc., or you can enlist Siri to help you.

Wrap Up

We've covered some of the more common personalization and customization options available in the Settings area. However, there are many more options and settings to explore. Before you move on, take a few minutes and go through the Settings menu item-by-item, just to see what's there. This is a great way to really take control of your iPhone - even if you don't change anything, knowing your options will go a long way toward making you an iPhone expert.

Part 5: Maintenance and Security

Now that you've spent so much time learning how to use your iPhone and how to set it up to perfectly suit your needs, you'll want to be sure that all that effort won't go to waste. This chapter will share some tips for keeping your iPhone safe from harm.

5.1 Maintenance

Your iPhone requires very little maintenance, but there are a few things you can do to keep it happy and healthy.

Cleaning

It's a good idea to clean your iPhone regularly to keep your screen clear and the touchscreen functioning. The iPhone screen is oleophobic, meaning it resists fingerprints, but you'll find it tends to get a little a smudged. Excessive grime can also interfere with the touchscreen's responsiveness.

Use a microfiber cloth and specialized screen cleaning fluid (NOT other household cleaners or water) to gently wipe the screen every so often.

Case

iPhones are fairly tough, but not indestructible, particularly with regard to their glass screens. They're also not cheap. It's a good idea to find a case to help protect it from falls. Just be sure to buy a case designed for the iPhone 8 or iPhone 8 Plus. Due to the larger screen size of these models, they won't work with cases designed for earlier models like iPhone 4 or the iPhone 5 series. There are plenty of cases out there for every budget and lifestyle, including waterproof and shatterproof designs.

Battery

Nothing puts a damper on an iPhone session quicker than having to scramble for a source of power. While the iPhone 8 has the longest battery life of any iPhone model to date and iOS 10 includes all kinds of under-the-hood improvements that extend it even further, follow these tips to make the battery last as long as possible if you'll be away from a power source for an extended period of time.

Battery Basics

"Battery life" refers to the amount of time your iPhone will run before it must be recharged. To help your battery life last, be sure to put your iPhone into lock mode when you are not using it, and get in the habit of charging it often. Plugging the iPhone into a wall will charge it much faster than merely charging through a computer's USB port. In fact, leaving it plugged in to a hibernating computer may actually drain the battery.

Use it (up) or lose it

Every few weeks, it's a good idea to let your battery drain all the way to the bottom of its charge. This keeps your iPhone from giving you inaccurate reads on remaining battery life.

Update, Update, Update!

Keep your iPhone system updated to the latest software version, and keep your apps updated as well. While the app content and user interface may not change, app updates often improve performance and battery usage. So don't be lazy – keep your apps and operating system up to date!

Settings

If you have the ability to regularly charge your iPhone, you may not worry about battery life too much. However, if you have limited access to power sources, making a few tweaks to settings or disabling unnecessary apps will reduce your iPhone's energy consumption and help maximize battery life.

- Low Power Mode: iOS 10 has a way to conserve battery called Low Power Mode. Your iPhone will notify you when your battery dips below 20%, and it will ask if you'd like to turn Low Power Mode on. Alternatively, you can enable it in Settings > Battery. This won't disable any major functionality, but it will reduce or turn off fetch and push processes and automatic downloads.

- Airplane Mode: Use this mode, which turns off your Wi-Fi, Bluetooth and 3G/LTE, whenever you don't need those functions to be active. Go to Settings > Airplane Mode > On or use the Control Center. Your iPhone uses battery life to connect to Wi-Fi and LTE, and the weaker the connection, the more battery life it can end up using to keep that connection active (or to search for a signal if the connection is lost). LTE is especially a battery hog!

- Push notifications and fetch data: Some applications use push notifications to send alerts or frequently fetch data (Mail, for example). The more frequently data is fetched or push notifications are sent, the faster your battery may drain, as this uses energy to continually update. Changing your fetch settings to every hour (rather than every few minutes) reduces energy consumption. These settings are located in Settings > (App Name).

- Background app refresh and cellular data: Many apps are set by default to refresh themselves whether or not they're being used (Facebook, Gmail, etc.). You can turn this off in Settings > (App Name). Alternatively, you can bulk edit this setting in Settings > General > Background App Refresh. Here you can turn it off altogether or turn it off app by app. Many apps that rely on streaming (Podcasts, Music) can also be set to only stream over Wi-Fi and not LTE, which is potentially expensive both in terms of battery use and your data plan!

- Minimize Location Services: Applications that use location services, which pinpoint your current location on a map, will drain the battery faster. To reduce consumption, go to Settings > General > Location Services and use location services only when needed.

- Dim it down and keep it cool: You can change brightness to a lower setting either in Settings > Wallpaper and Brightness or straight from your Control Center (swipe up from the bottom of the screen to access it). Using only as much brightness as you need will help your battery last longer. It will also keep your battery from overheating.

- Monitor your apps: iOS 10 lets you see exactly which apps are draining your battery the most. Visit Settings > Battery to see which apps have consumed the largest percentage of your battery life over either the last 24 hours or over the last seven days. When your battery's running low, you can use this information to help it last a little longer by avoiding your really power-hungry apps.

Temperature

Like humans, the iPhone will function in temperatures ranging from 32 to 95 degrees Fahrenheit, but it's happiest at 72 degrees (room temperature). Be very careful with extreme heat and cold; they can ruin your iPhone if you're not careful. Be especially careful about leaving your device in the car – if it's too hot to leave a baby or a dog in a vehicle, don't leave your iPhone in one either!

Keep in mind that charging your iPhone while it is in certain carrying cases may generate excessive heat, which can affect battery capacity. If you notice that your iPhone gets hot when you charge it, take it out of its case first.

5.2 Security

There are a few things you can do to help secure your iPhone, and iOS 10 includes serious improvements in security. Setting up Find My iPhone during setup is a good start, but if you need to further secure your device, here are three other powerful options.

Setting a Passcode

To set a passcode that must be entered every time your iPhone turns on or wakes up (if you haven't already during the initial setup process), go to Settings > Touch ID & Passcode. Tap Turn Passcode On and enter a six-digit password of your choosing.

Screenshot 148: Setting a Passcode and the Passcode Lock Screen

iPhone defaults to a simple passcode of six numbers. If you prefer to use the old four-digit passcode, tap Passcode Options and then tap 4-Digit Numeric Code. Just keep in mind that there are 10,000 possible four-digit combinations compared to one million six-digit combinations. If you're really cautious, choose Custom Alphanumeric Code or Custom Numeric Code, which will give you more leeway in designing your passcode. You can also set your iPhone to erase all of its data if more than ten incorrect passcodes are entered – do NOT do this if you're unsure about your ability to remember your passcode! You can adjust the length of time before a passcode will be required again, though we recommend leaving it set to the default setting – immediately.

Touch ID (Fingerprints)

Your iPhone 8 or iPhone 8 Plus comes pre-equipped with a fingerprint scanner integrated into the enlarged Home button on the device. This means that you can set up your own unique fingerprint as a password for your phone. Simply pressing the Home button will authenticate you and unlock the phone in one nearly impossible to hack motion. You can also use this feature to authenticate App Store and iTunes purchases – no more poking out your Apple ID password!

Touch ID is easy to set up if you skipped this step during the initial iPhone setup process. Visit Settings > Touch ID & Passcode. Tap Add a Fingerprint and follow the instructions to set up your own unique fingerprint. The more often you use it, the more accurate it gets! We recommend adding both thumbs, as you can add more than one print to your phone.

Restrictions

Restrictions are useful settings for parents worried about their children's ability to run up the family credit card or for parents who want to control their child's access to certain features, like the Camera. To set restrictions, visit Settings > General > Restrictions.

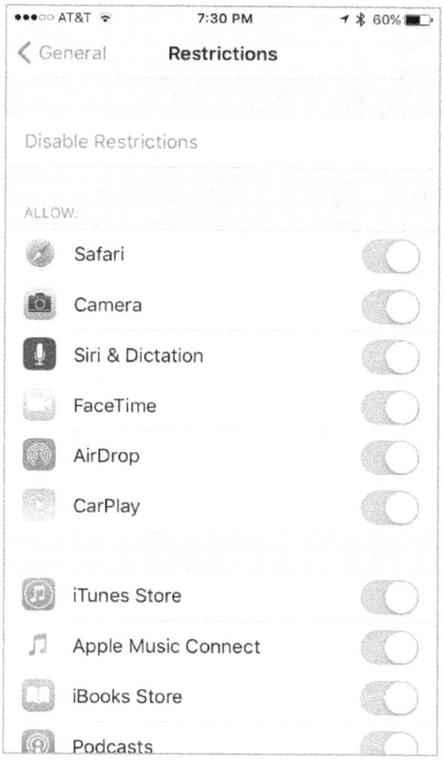

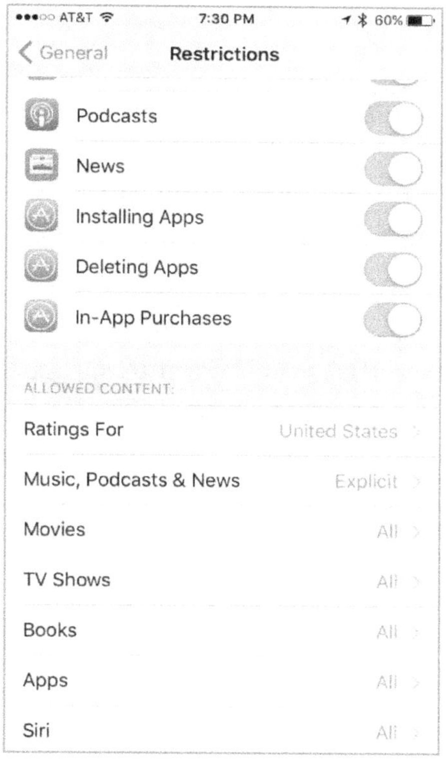

Screenshot 149: Setting Up Restrictions

Tap Enable Restrictions to get started. You'll be prompted for a four-digit restrictions passcode. After you set that up, you'll be able to prevent subsequent iPhone users from using Safari, iTunes, FaceTime, or any of the other apps listed in the Restrictions settings area. You can also filter for explicit language, allow or disallow in-app purchases, and set acceptable ratings for viewable content (e.g. movies with PG ratings). Parents can even set an audio volume limit to protect developing eardrums! We strongly recommend that parents and educators familiarize themselves with restrictions, for the well-being of their children and their bank accounts.

Guided Access

Guided Access may be useful for parents or educators who want to limit iPhone use to a single app. To use it, first you'll need to turn it on in Settings > General > Accessibility > Guided Access. After enabling Guided Access, tapping the Home button three times while in the app you want to limit the user to will activate Guided Access mode. You can set time limits in Guided Access as well, forcing the user to end his or her session after a duration of your choosing.

Wrap Up

It's easy to forget how much of a financial investment your iPhone 8 is, since you'll probably carry it with you everywhere. However, as convenient and easy to use as your iPhone is, it remains a highly sophisticated and fairly expensive electronic device, and you'll want to follow the suggestions outlined above to keep it safe! We also cannot stress the importance of security enough. iPhones get lost or worse, stolen, very frequently. Chances are, you'll load your own iPhone up with highly personal information that you'll want to safeguard should your iPhone fall into the wrong hands. Fortunately, thanks to the security features discussed above, it's easy to configure your iPhone so that a thief won't be able to make off with much besides a phone-shaped paperweight!

Part 6: Must-Have Apps for Your iPhone

You've no doubt heard Apple's catch phrase, "there's an app for that." And it's usually true! This section outlines fifty of our favorite apps, though with around 1.5 million apps available in the App Store, you're bound to discover hidden gems we haven't covered here.

Note: all prices are current as of 2017. However, like anything related to finances, they are subject to change.

6.1 Games

Games are one of the most popular categories of iPhone apps, and with good reason. Here are some of our favorite games for iPhone, but be warned: some of these pose a serious risk to your work, school, and sleep schedules.

2048 (Free)

We feel irresponsible even recommending this one, it's so absurdly addictive. It's a tile game whose goal is to create the number 2048 by doubling the numbers on tiles by matching them with each other. Don't say we didn't warn you.

Angry Birds (full version: $0.99 / Lite version: Free)

Angry Birds is a classic iPhone app that has helplessly addicted players since the very first iPhone. Game play is deceptively simple – launch a bird from a slingshot and cause enough to destruction to vanquish the evil green pigs. However, as you progress through the levels, you'll find yourself faced with increasingly difficult physics challenges. The game is available in a number of editions, including Angry Birds Seasons, Angry Birds Space, Angry Birds Rio and Angry Birds Star Wars.

Candy Crush Saga (Free)

This addictive and fun time-waster challenges players to over 300 puzzles. It's free, but includes inevitable in-app purchases.

Clash of Clans (Free)

Build your village, improve it by raiding other players' villages for resources, defend it from marauding players, and team up with others by joining a clan. This is a free, social game with in-app purchases.

Fruit Ninja (full version: $0.99 / Lite version: Free)

Use your finger to slice fruit with your ninja sword, best your high scores, and compete with friends. We couldn't tell you why this is so much fun, but trust us, it is.

Dots (Free)

This incredibly simple game requires players to connect series of colored dots. It's easy and each game play session only lasts 60 seconds. Of course, besting your increasingly high score becomes challenging. Let's just say that we've lost hours of our lives to this.

Draw Something (full version: $2.99 / ad-supported: Free)

Find friends to play with and guess each other's art! This is a low stakes game that's a great avenue for creativity and frequent hilarity.

Monument Valley (3.99)

Journey through a gorgeously designed M.C. Escher- esque world, solving puzzles that defy our understanding of space. Perfect for all ages.

Plants versus Zombies 2: It's About Time (Free)

The blockbuster original Plants versus Zombies game returns in this sequel for FREE, with in-app purchases. Built on a classic tower defense gameplay model, PVZ adds bizarre and hilarious characters as the player pits weaponized botany against legions of the undead. This sequel adds a time travel component that results in maps in Ancient Egypt, a pirate ship, the Old West, and the Middle Ages for starters.

Pokemon Go (Free)

If you haven't already downloaded this game, you'll definitely want to. But, be warned, it's addicting for players of all ages. Catch your favorite Pokemon while walking and exploring outside. If competitive gameplay is more your speed, battle it out with other Pokemon to support your team – all with your favorite Pokemon by your side.

Words With Friends (full version: $2.99/ ad-supported: Free)

Challenge your friends to a match in this word-lover's Scrabble-style game.

6.2 Reading and News Apps

In addition to your iPhone's onboard News and iBooks apps, you can download several apps that expand the reading material available on iPhone.

Comixology (Free)

If you're a comic book fan, this is an essential app. Its Guided View feature lets you move from panel to panel naturally. The app is free, but the comics usually cost money. Set up an account with Comixology to buy comics at the Comixology website and then read them using this app. It's easy and impressively close to reading a dead tree comic. The selection is reasonable, and includes Marvel, DC, Vertigo and Image titles, among others.

Dark Sky ($3.99)

This award-winning ultra-local weather app lets you know with amazing specificity *exactly* when it's going to rain at your precise location. If you find yourself squinting at the radar map, try this one. It's scarily good at what it does.

Flipboard (free)

Flipboard presents your Facebook, Twitter, Tumblr, Sound Cloud and other content in a beautiful magazine layout. It's a great way to consolidate your information feeds into one aesthetically pleasing interface that's perfect for flipping through.

Nook (Free)

Turn your iPhone into a Nook eReader with the Nook app from Barnes and Noble. Sign in with your Barnes and Noble account to have Nook books wirelessly delivered to your iPhone. It's easy to use and the Nook library is huge.

Kindle (Free)

The Kindle app will allow you to download ebooks from Amazon's Kindle store.

NPR (Free)

The magazine-style user-interface of this app emphasizes news, arts, lifestyle and music coverage. You can access hundreds of NPR live stations (searchable by GPS or ZIP code) and on-demand broadcast streams, and create a playlist of stories to save for later. Enjoy stunning photojournalism with full-page zoom, and share stories via e-mail, Twitter and Facebook.

Overdrive (Free)

Check with your local public library to see if it subscribes to Overdrive. If so, this free app will let you download free library ebooks and audiobooks to your iPhone.

Reuters News Pro (Free)

This app puts you at the pulse of Reuter's venerable newswire. Customize your daily feed by choosing from dozens of categories, create a specific list for business news, and further customize with geographic-specific newsfeeds.

The Weather Channel (Free)

If you need more weather information than the native Weather app can give, definitely install the official Weather Channel app. It's a very well presented and highly informative tool.

6.3 Music, TV and Movies

Fandango (Free)

This Wallet-ready app will help you find movies near you and purchase tickets.

Flixter (Free)

Movie lovers will want Flixter, which includes reviews from Rotten Tomatoes and finds movie theaters near you, along with show times, trailers and more.

Hulu Plus (Free)

If you have a Hulu Plus account, you'll want access on your iPhone. The app is free to install, but the actual Hulu Plus subscription is paid.

Netflix (Free)

If you subscribe to Netflix, this is an essential app! The iPhone is perfect for streaming movies, and the Netflix app is easy to use. Just sign in with your account and start watching.

Pandora (Free)

The pioneer of Internet radio is now available at a flick of your fingertips. The user interface also features a few improvements over the existing computer version; it displays a sliding panel of albums, your playlists, and detailed artist info as each track plays. If you've already got a Pandora account set up, you'll want to install the app to gain access to your stations. Otherwise, you might as well just use iTunes Radio.

Spotify (Free, paid subscription optional)

Spotify is another streaming music service that's worth your attention. You can play any artist, album or playlist you like, for free.

6.4 Productivity

Dropbox (Free)

Dropbox is a really useful tool for moving files from computer to computer, especially if one of those computers is a Windows computer. Install the free app, register for a free Dropbox account, and you're ready to take advantage of very easy-to-use cloud storage. You can also install the Dropbox program on your computer, or just head to Dropbox.com to access your files from any internet connection. Dropbox is also a great way to transfer photos from your phone.

Evernote (Free)

Change the way you take notes; never forget an important message or an unexpected, special moment. Turn snippets from blogs, recorded sounds and graphic images or photos into digital notes. View and access all your notes with a few swipes of your finger, quickly find the notes you need with 'tag' view, and use the map to geo-tag your notes. Syncs automatically over a Wi-Fi or 3G connection with your desktop Evernote and your tablet Evernote.

Google Chrome (Free)

Safari has greatly improved in iOS 10, but if you're too deeply entangled in Google's browser, you'll be able to access your stored Google data and other Chromey goodness on your iPhone as well.

LastPass (Free with a paid LastPass subscription)

LastPass with Safari and Touch ID integration is a miracle in this age of high-profile password hacks. LastPass is a password manager and it's one of the finest around. With LastPass Premium you get access to the LastPass iOS app and Safari browser extension. Imagine only needing to remember one password while maintaining extremely secure and unique passwords for every single account in your life. We can't recommend this one enough, and at $12 a year, the subscription is not unreasonably priced.

iWork Suite: Numbers, Pages and Keynote (Free)

iWork applications are Apple's answer to Microsoft Office, but Apple offers them for free for iOS users. Jump on this – iWork is world-class office software, and its integration with iCloud means you can access your documents, spreadsheets and presentations anywhere you've got an internet connection.

Wunderlist (Free)

If you're a serious list maker, you'll want to install this free cloud-based list system. Wunderlist gives you serious flexibility and collaboration options, making it a beefier, cross-platform-compatible alternative to your iPhone's Notes and Reminders apps.

6.5 Education

DuoLingo (Free)

DuoLingo is a language-learning app that gamifies language acquisition. It's fun, easy and a great way to get started with a foreign language.

Google Earth (Free)

Google Earth is a highly accurate virtual map and so much more! As a digital globe, it allows you to not only zoom in on specific places, but you can also take 3D tours of entire cities. In recent versions, you can even take 3D virtual tours of museums, monuments, and other landmarks. In recent versions, you can even explore the bottom of the ocean and the surface of Mars. Google Earth is a must-have app for your iPhone.

Google Translate (Free)

The Google Translate app is wonderful for traveling or language study. Of course, you can't rely on it to construct sentences that don't sound machine-translated, but it's a great quick way to look up a word in a foreign language on the fly.

Star Walk ($2.99)

This app is a good choice for demonstrating the awesomeness of the iPhone. Use it to view the labeled night sky. Location Services allow you to point your iPhone in any direction (including down) to see what's going on in the galaxy. The 360-degree view of the universe is breathtaking. If you're only going to buy one app, we can't recommend this one enough.

Wikipanion (Free)

This app puts the world's collective knowledge at your fingertips, distilling Wikipedia's content into an iPhone-friendly viewing pane and easy-to-use interface. Save images you find to your iPhone's photo library and bookmark your favorite searches. If you truly love the app, you may want to upgrade to the Plus version for $2.99; you'll enjoy faster page load speeds and will be able to save pages for offline reading at a later time.

6.6 Creative Tools

Adobe Vector Draw (Free)

Your new digital sketchbook allows you to capture and explore ideas no matter where you are when inspiration strikes. Combining classic elements from Adobe Photoshop and Illustrator, such as layers, brushes, and undo/redo, Adobe Vector Draw (which replaced Adobe Ideas) upgrades your drawings from pixilated scribbles to artistic sketches. The best part? No graphic design background is required!

Epicurious (Free)

The premier app for foodies, the easy-to-use interface turns your iPhone into a luxury cookbook featuring over 30,000 recipes. Save favorite recipes, add ingredients to a shopping list, and search for recipes by main ingredients, course, cuisine, dietary restrictions, season and occasion. With gorgeous graphics, you may find yourself drooling over the amazing dishes!

Photoshop Express (Free)

This is a very, very abbreviated version of Adobe's famous photo editing software, but it will allow you to do some basic fixes that you can't do in the Photos app.

6.7 Social Apps

Instagram (Free)

If you find yourself taking and sharing photos with any kind of frequency, you'll enjoy Instagram. You can sync it with Facebook and Twitter for effortless photo sharing. There are also a number of filter effects that can add a creative twist to your pictures!

Pinterest, Facebook, Twitter, YouTube, Vimeo, et al. (Free)

Most major online platforms include a free app, which typically provides a much richer experience than what's available in a mobile browser. If there's a service you find yourself using daily, check the App Store to see if there's an appified version!

Skype (Free)

The Skype app is a great alternative to FaceTime if you have friends and family who haven't jumped on the Apple bandwagon (yet). Skype video calls are just as free and just as high quality as their FaceTime counterparts.

Snapchat (Free)

Snapchat has a bit of an image problem, due to well-publicized illicit uses for this fun disposable messaging app, but it's actually quite a bit of fun to use for innocuous purposes. Snapchats self-destruct after viewing, making it a silly and fun way to share short video bursts without running up anybody's storage use. We should stress though that Snapchat is not particularly secure and anything you send using it could be reproduced as a screenshot or screencast.

WordPress (Free)

Create, save and publish posts and pages for your WordPress blog directly from your iPhone.

Yelp (Free)

Check local reviews wherever you go for advice on restaurants, activities and services. Search for a specific business or general service, check hours and narrow search results by neighborhood, price and distance.

6.8 Lifestyle

Breeze (Free)

This pedometer app from the makers of Runkeeper keeps track of your steps for you passively. It gathers data from the M8 motion coprocessor chip in your phone, and displays your steps in a more aesthetically pleasing format than the Health app. It also sets goals for you based on your average number of steps and sends you encouraging notifications throughout the day.

Kayak (Free)

Quickly search across most major airlines for airfare prices, with a simple interface for picking start/end dates, destinations and a date range. Set up airfare price alerts and be notified when fares drop.

MyFitnessPal (Free)

MyFitnessPal is an excellent calorie counter app that makes watching what you eat painless (er, relatively painless). You can search for most foods to automatically add nutritional information or simply scan barcodes. Add your calories burned through exercise and stay on track to meet your weight loss and/or health goals.

Runkeeper (Free)

Track your exercise, including distance covered, calories burned, average speed, etc. While it's obviously great for runners, you can use it to log other fitness activities too!

ShopStyle (Free)

ShopStyle is an elegant shopping app that includes over 300 retailers. Fun to use, and potentially very dangerous if you're trying to not to spend money.

Shpock (Free)

If you like garage sales and classified ads, run don't walk to download this sale finder app.

Trulia (Free)

Find your dream home with Trulia's real estate finder for iPhone. Search by location, save searches, view photos, reviews, and more. A must-have app for anyone looking for a home.

Wrap Up

We hope these apps have given you some ideas using your iPhone! If none of the above caught your fancy, think about what you enjoy. Try finding it in the App Store – there are apps for musicians, writers, computer programmers, parents, etc., and there's bound to be something just for you

Conclusion

By now, you should be ready to use your iPhone like a pro. You know how to get around and make the most of your pre-installed apps, how to customize your settings, how to take care of your iPhone, and how to find new apps to help you get the most out of iPhone 8 and iOS 10.

We hope you've enjoyed getting to know your iPhone. There's so much more to explore, though, and as you become more familiar with your device, you'll discover new and exciting ways to use it that we've never even dreamed of. Those possibilities are just part of the fun of owning an iOS mobile device. As you continue to use your iPhone, you'll find ways to adapt your iPhone to your unique personality and lifestyle. With the information in this guide, you now have a solid foundation to build on, and we hope your iPhone brings you years of entertainment, education, productivity and usefulness.

Good luck and have fun!

www.ingramcontent.com/pod-product-compliance
Lightning Source LLC
Chambersburg PA
CBHW080811280726
48660CB00018B/3206
9781979344371